'06

Career and Academic
Advising Center

INTERNET

Third Edition

Ferguson
An imprint of Infobase Publishing

Careers in Focus: Internet, Third Edition

Copyright © 2006 by Infobase Publishing

Ferguson
An imprint of Infobase Publishing
132 West 31st Street
New York NY 10001

Library of Congress Cataloging-in-Publication Data

Careers in focus. Internet. — 3rd ed.
     p. cm.
   Includes index.
   ISBN 0-8160-6564-0 (hc : alk. paper)
   1. Internet—Vocational guidance—Juvenile literature. 2. Webmasters—Juvenile literature. 3. Computer programming—Vocational guidance—Juvenile literature. 4. Telecommunications—Vocational guidance—Juvenile literature. I. Title: Internet.
   TK5105.875.I57C369 2006
   004.67′802373—dc22   2006008402

Ferguson books are available at special discounts when purchased in bulk quantities for businesses, associations, institutions, or sales promotions. Please call our Special Sales Department in New York at (212) 967-8800 or (800) 322-8755.

You can find Ferguson on the World Wide Web at http://www.fergpubco.com

Text design by David Strelecky

Printed in the United States of America

MP Hermitage 10 9 8 7 6 5 4 3 2 1

This book is printed on acid-free paper.

Table of Contents

Introduction

Perhaps you're a casual user of the Internet, occasionally surfing the Web and sending email. Perhaps you've published your own Web page and spend several hours a day online reading the latest news, checking stock quotes, buying groceries, doing research for a paper, or playing computer games. Regardless of your experience with the Internet, your future will be affected by its existence.

The Internet is a worldwide network of computer networks linked together through high-speed, high-volume telephone lines and cables, as well as via wireless connection (known as Wi-Fi). You can use it to talk to someone in India, buy salsa from someone in Texas, check the status of your stock portfolio, learn about colon cancer, or chat with a group of people about your common interest in hip-hop music.

Today's Internet bears little resemblance to its beginnings. In 1958, Russia launched *Sputnik,* and the Cold War was in full swing. Soon after, the Advanced Research Projects Agency (ARPA) was created by the U.S. Department of Defense to help the United States regain and maintain a lead in technology. The Department of Defense wanted a comprehensive, indestructible network that could communicate even when under enemy attack. If one of the computer links was destroyed, messages still had to be able to get through to their destination. With this in mind, packet switching was developed in 1968. Within a message (packet) was information about its destination and how to get there so that, if it hit a point of failure in its route, the message could tell where it needed to go next to reach its final destination.

In 1969, using packet switching, ARPA created an internetwork (a network of networks) called ARPANET. There was still a problem, however. How could they get different types of networks to communicate with one another? The U.S. military wanted to link all their networks together worldwide. Despite its inability to link these different networks together, the ARPANET grew. Military and defense contractors, universities, and scientists were rapidly getting connected to this internetwork. Throughout the 1970s and 1980s, different portions of ARPANET were declassified and opened up to the public. The first public demonstration of ARPANET occurred in 1972, and other organizations began asking permission to connect their networks to it. In 1983, a new protocol (a way computers talk to each other) called Transmission Control Protocol/Internet Protocol

(TCP/IP) was integrated into ARPANET and the all-inclusive network finally was realized. Many Internet historians cite ARPANET's switching over to TCP/IP as the birth of the Internet.

In 1986, the National Science Foundation began NSFNET, a much faster network than ARPANET, which connected five super-computing centers at Princeton University, the University of Pittsburgh, the University of California-San Diego, the University of Illinois-Urbana-Champaign, and Cornell University. The purpose was to connect major researchers and scientists around the globe. These five quickly grew to include more universities and some corporations and industrial institutions, including the National Aeronautics and Space Administration. Soon, email, file transfer, and newsgroups became commonplace. By 1990, due to a newer, faster NSFNET, ARPANET was disbanded and commercial (business for profit) use was permitted on NSFNET.

Because NSFNET was largely funded through federal grants, the network was becoming too costly for the U.S. government. So by 1993, commercial firms stepped in and provided faster and higher capacity transmission, and the Internet became more efficient. The lines put in place by this faster network became the backbone (the main arteries of the Internet where the largest volume of messaging traffic travels) for today's Internet. NSFNET was shut down in 1995 because the Internet had grown to assume all of NSFNET's abilities and more.

ARPANET and NSFNET were based in the United States, but at the same time they were being developed, across the globe other networks were popping up in different regions. For example, the EBONE, which was created in 1991, as a group of European organizations coordinated their efforts to form their own internetwork. EBONE soon plugged into the U.S. Internet backbone and suddenly Europe and the United States were linked together. This has happened worldwide to such an extent that today every country on every continent has Internet access.

The World Wide Web was the brainchild of physicist Tim Berners-Lee (born in 1955), who developed a way to organize information in a more logical fashion by using hypertext to link portions of documents to one another. Although Berners-Lee formed his idea of the Web in 1989, it was another four years before the first Web browser (Mosaic) made it possible for people to navigate the Web simply.

No one person or organization is in charge of the Internet and what's on it. Various organizations take part in its administration. For example, the Internet Corporation of Assigned Names and Numbers (ICANN), a nonprofit, private corporation, is responsible for coordinating the assignment of Internet domain names, IP address numbers, and protocol parameter and port numbers. As part of this work, ICANN accredits registrars offering .com, .net, .org, .biz, and other top-level domain names. The Internet Society, a non-profit, nongovernmental, and international organization, works to maintain the global viability of the Internet by focusing on technical standards, public policies, and education and training. The World Wide Web Consortium (W3C) promotes the development of common protocols to ensure global usability of the Web. No organization controls the Internet, however.

As an industry, the Internet is one of the most dynamic and evolving sectors of the U.S.—and the world—economy. Growth in the use of the Internet has been phenomenal. While it is difficult to come up with exact figures, Nua Internet Surveys estimates that in the United States alone the number of Internet users went from approximately 18 million in 1995 to some 164 million in 2002.

Job possibilities in cyberspace are practically endless. Naturally, crossover exists between the computer field and the Internet field since the Internet developed from computer applications. Some traditional computer professionals (for example, computer engineers, software designers, computer programmers, and database specialists) continue to focus their work on supporting and enhancing the functioning of the Internet. Internet professionals as a group, however, include more than these computer workers. For example, there is the consultant who builds websites for clients, the advertiser who creates ads to show on websites, and the writer whose columns appear in online magazines. One way to think of this field is by dividing Internet workers into two general categories: those who make (or build) the Internet, and those who make use of the Internet.

Professionals who make the Internet include, but are not limited to, the following: Internet developers, Internet consultants, Internet quality assurance specialists, Internet transaction specialists, and webmasters. Examples of workers who make use of the Internet include online journalists, online producers, information brokers, graphics programmers, and computer and video game designers.

As the Internet continues to grow in popularity, speed, strength, and uses, the differences between these two general categories of workers will undoubtedly become less distinct. While no one can say with certainty where the Internet will take us, it is clear that more and more professionals will become involved in both making and making use of the Internet.

There is a huge variety of possibilities for cyberspace careers. Perhaps no other industry is expected to offer as many diverse opportunities. Internet growth will increase employment opportunities with computer and network hardware suppliers, access providers, software companies, Internet consulting firms, and e-commerce developers. There is a continuing need for skilled computer science workers and a rapidly growing market for designers and managers who can combine Internet savvy and know-how with their ability to create, produce, and manage Web content.

Each article in this book discusses a particular Internet occupation in detail. The articles in *Careers in Focus: Internet* appear in Ferguson's *Encyclopedia of Careers and Vocational Guidance,* but have been updated and revised with the latest information from the U.S. Department of Labor, professional organizations, and other sources. The following paragraphs detail the sections and features that appear in the book.

The **Quick Facts** section provides a brief summary of the career, including recommended school subjects, personal skills, work environment, minimum educational requirements, salary ranges, certification or licensing requirements, and employment outlook. This section also provides acronyms and identification numbers for the following government classification indexes: the *Dictionary of Occupational Titles* (DOT), the *Guide for Occupational Exploration* (GOE), the National Occupational Classification (NOC) Index, and the Occupational Information Network (O*NET)-Standard Occupational Classification System (SOC) index. The DOT, GOE, and O*NET-SOC indexes have been created by the U.S. government; the NOC index is Canada's career classification system. Readers can use the identification numbers listed in the Quick Facts section to access further information about a career. Print editions of the DOT (*Dictionary of Occupational Titles.* Indianapolis, Ind.: JIST Works, 1991) and GOE (*The Guide for Occupational Exploration.* 3d ed. Indianapolis, Ind.: JIST Works, 2001) are available at libraries. Electronic versions of the NOC (http://www23.hrdc-drhc.gc.ca) and O*NET-SOC (http://online.onetcenter.org) are available on the World Wide Web. When no DOT, GOE, NOC, or O*NET-SOC numbers are present, this means that the U.S. Department of Labor or Human Resources Development Canada have not created a numerical designation for this career. In this instance, you will see the acronym "N/A," or not available.

The **Overview** section is a brief introductory description of the duties and responsibilities involved in this career. Oftentimes, a career may have a variety of job titles. When this is the case, alternative career titles are presented.

The **History** section describes the history of the particular job as it relates to the overall development of its industry or field.

The Job describes the primary and secondary duties of the job.

Requirements discusses high school and postsecondary education and training requirements, any certification or licensing that is necessary, and other personal requirements for success in the job.

Exploring offers suggestions on how to gain experience in or knowledge of the particular job before making a firm educational and financial commitment. The focus is on what can be done while still in high school (or in the early years of college) to gain a better understanding of the job.

The **Employers** section gives an overview of typical places of employment for the job.

Starting Out discusses the best ways to land that first job, be it through the college placement office, newspaper ads, or personal contact.

The **Advancement** section describes what kind of career path to expect from the job and how to get there.

Earnings lists salary ranges and describes the typical fringe benefits.

The **Work Environment** section describes the typical surroundings and conditions of employment—whether indoors or outdoors, noisy or quiet, social or independent. Also discussed are typical hours worked, any seasonal fluctuations, and the stresses and strains of the job.

The **Outlook** section summarizes the job in terms of the general economy and industry projections. For the most part, Outlook information is obtained from the U.S. Bureau of Labor Statistics and is supplemented by information taken from professional associations. Job growth terms follow those used in the *Occupational Outlook Handbook*. Growth described as "much faster than the average" means an increase of 36 percent or more. Growth described as "faster than the average" means an increase of 21 to 35 percent. Growth described as "about as fast as the average" means an increase of 10 to 20 percent. Growth described as "more slowly than the average" means an increase of 3 to 9 percent. Growth described as "little or no change" means an increase of 0 to 2 percent. "Decline" means a decrease of 1 percent or more. Each article ends with **For More Information,** which lists organizations that provide information on training, education, internships, scholarships, and job placement.

Careers in Focus: Internet also includes photos, informative sidebars, and interviews with professionals in the field.

Computer and Video Game Designers

QUICK FACTS

School Subjects
Art
Computer science

Personal Skills
Communication/ideas
Technical/scientific

Work Environment
Primarily indoors
Primarily one location

Minimum Education Level
Bachelor's degree

Salary Range
$41,652 to $53,031 to
$300,000

Certification or Licensing
None available

Outlook
About as fast as the average

DOT
N/A

GOE
N/A

NOC
2174

O*NET-SOC
27-1029.99

OVERVIEW

In the sector of the multibillion-dollar computer industry known as interactive entertainment and recreational computing, *computer and video game designers* create the ideas and interactivity for games. These games work on various platforms, or media, such as video consoles and computers, and through online Internet subscriptions. They generate ideas for new game concepts, including sound effects, characters, story lines, and graphics.

Because the industry is fairly new, it is difficult to estimate how many people work as game designers. Around 90,000 people work within the video game industry as a whole. Designers either work for companies that make the games or create the games on their own and sell their ideas and programs to companies that produce them.

HISTORY

Computer and video game designers are a relatively new breed. The industry didn't begin to develop until the 1960s and 1970s, when computer programmers at some large universities, big companies, and government labs began designing games on mainframe computers. Steve Russell was perhaps the first video game designer. In 1962, when he was in college, he made up a simple game called *Spacewar*. Graphics of space ships flew through a starry sky on the video screen, the object of the game being to shoot down enemy ships. Nolan Bushnell, another early designer, played *Spacewar* in college. In 1972 he put the first video game in an arcade; it was a game very much like

6

Spacewar, and he called it *Computer Space.* However, many users found the game difficult to play, so it wasn't a success.

Bruce Artwick published the first of many versions of *Flight Simulator,* and Bushnell later created *Pong,* a game that required the players to paddle electronic ping-pong balls back and forth across the video screen. *Pong* was a big hit, and players spent thousands of quarters in arcade machines all over the country playing it. Bushnell's company, Atari, had to hire more and more designers every week, including Steve Jobs, Alan Kay, and Chris Crawford. These early designers made games with text-based descriptions (that is, no graphics) of scenes and actions with interactivity done through a computer keyboard. Games such as *Adventure, Star Trek,* and *Flight Simulator* were among the first that designers created. They used simple commands like "look at building" and "move west." Most games were designed for video machines; not until the later 1970s did specially equipped TVs and early personal computers (PCs) begin appearing.

In the late 1970s and early 1980s, designers working for Atari and Intellivision made games for home video systems, PCs, and video arcades. Many of these new games had graphics, sound, text, and animation. Designers of games like *Pac-Man, Donkey Kong,* and *Space Invaders* were successful and popular. They also started to make role-playing games like the famous *Dungeons and Dragons.* Richard Garriott created *Ultima,* another major role-playing game. Games began to feature the names and photos of their programmers on the packaging, giving credit to individual designers.

Workers at Electronic Arts began to focus on making games for PCs to take advantage of technology that included the computer keyboard, more memory, and floppy disks. They created games like *Carmen Sandiego* and *M.U.L.E.* In the mid- to late 1980s, new technology included more compact floppies, sound cards, and larger memory. Designers also had to create games that would work on more than just one platform—PCs, Apple computers, and 64-bit video game machines.

In the 1990s, Electronic Arts started to hire teams of designers instead of "lone wolf" individuals (those who design games from start to finish independently). Larger teams were needed because games became more complex; design teams would include not only programmers but also artists, musicians, writers, and animators. Designers made such breakthroughs as using more entertaining graphics, creating more depth in role-playing games, using virtual reality in sports games, and using more visual realism in racing games and flight simulators. This new breed of designers created games using techniques like Assembly, C, and HyperCard. By 1994, designers began to use CD-ROM technology to its fullest. In only a few months, *Doom* was a hit. Designers of this game gave players the chance to alter the game at various levels, including choices of weapons and enemies. *Doom* still has fans worldwide.

The success of shareware (software that is given away to attract users to purchase a more complete version of the same software) has influenced the return of smaller groups of designers. Even the lone wolf is coming back, using shareware and better authoring tools such as sound libraries and complex multimedia development environments. Some designers are finding that they work best on their own or in small teams.

What's on the horizon for game designers? More multiplayer games; virtual reality; improved technology in coprocessors, chips, hardware, and sound fonts; and "persistent worlds," where online games are influenced by and evolve from players' actions. These new types of games require that designers know more and more complex code so that games can "react" to their multiple players.

THE JOB

Designing games involves programming code as well as creating stories, graphics, and sound effects. It is a very creative process, requiring imagination and computer and communication skills to develop games that are interactive and entertaining. As mentioned earlier, some game designers work on their own and try to sell their designs to companies that produce and distribute games; others are employees of companies such as Electronic Arts, Broderbund, and many others. Whether designers work alone or for a company, their aim is to create games that get players involved. Game players want to have fun, be challenged, and sometimes learn something along the way.

Each game must have a story line as well as graphics and sound that will entertain and engage the players. Story lines are situations that the players will find themselves in and make decisions about. Designers develop a plan for combining the story or concept, music or other sound effects, and graphics. They design rules to make it fun, challenging, or educational, and they create characters for the stories or circumstances, worlds in which these characters live, and problems or situations these characters will face.

One of the first steps is to identify the audience that will be playing the game. How old are the players? What kinds of things are they interested in? What kind of game will it be: action, adventure, "edutainment," role-playing, or sports? And which platform will the game use: video game system (e.g., Nintendo), computer (e.g., Macintosh), or online (Internet via subscription)?

The next steps are to create a design proposal, a preliminary design, and a final game design. The proposal is a brief summary of what the game involves. The preliminary design goes much further, outlining in more detail what the concept is (the story of the game); how the players get involved; what sound effects, graphics, and other elements will be included (What will the screen look like? What kinds of sound effects should the player hear?); and what productivity tools (such as word processors, database programs, spreadsheet programs, flowcharting programs, and prototyping programs) the designer intends to use to create these elements. Independent designers submit a product idea and design proposal to a publisher along with a cover letter and resume. Employees work as part of a team to create the proposal and design. Teamwork might include brainstorming sessions to come up with ideas, as well as involvement in market research (surveying the players who will be interested in the game).

The final game design details the basic idea, the plot, and every section of the game, including the startup process, all the scenes (such as innings for baseball games and maps for edutainment games), and all the universal elements (such as rules for scoring, names of characters, and a sound effect that occurs every time something specific happens). The story, characters, worlds, and maps are documented. The game design also includes details of the logic of the game, its algorithms (the step-by-step procedures for solving the problems the players will encounter), and its rules; the methods the player will use to load the game, start it up, score, win, lose, save, stop, and play again; the graphic design, including storyboards and sample art; and the audio design. The designer might also include marketing ideas and proposed follow-up games.

Designers interact with other workers and technologists involved in the game design project, including programmers, audio engineers, artists, and even *asset managers*, who coordinate the collecting, engineering, and distribution of physical assets to the *production team* (the people who will actually produce the physical CD-ROM or DVD).

Designers need to understand games and their various forms, think up new ideas, and experiment with and evaluate new designs. They assemble the separate elements (text, art, sound, video) of a game into a complete, interactive form, following through with careful planning and preparation (such as sketching out scripts, storyboards, and design documents). They write an implementation plan and guidelines (How will designers manage the process? How much will it cost to design the game? How long will the guidelines be—five pages? 300?). Finally, they amend designs at every stage, solving problems and answering questions.

Computer and video game designers often keep scrapbooks, notes, and journals of interesting ideas and other bits of information. They collect potential game material and even catalog ideas, videos, movies, pictures, stories, character descriptions, music clips, sound effects, animation sequences, and interface techniques. The average time to design a game, including all the elements and stages just described, can be from about six to 18 months.

REQUIREMENTS

High School
Playing video or computer games is one of the most important ways to become familiar with this type of work. You will also need to learn a programming language like C++ or Java, and you'll need a good working knowledge of the hardware platform for which you plan to develop your games (video, computer, online). In high school, learn as much as you can about computers: how they work, what kinds there are, how to program them, and any languages you can learn. You should also take physics, chemistry, and computer science. Since designers are creative, take courses such as art, literature, and music as well.

Postsecondary Training
Although strictly speaking you don't have to have a college degree to be a game designer, most companies are looking for creative people who also have a degree. Having one represents that you've been actively involved in intense, creative work; that you can work with others and follow through on assignments; and, of course, that you've learned what there is to know about programming, computer architecture (including input devices, processing devices, memory and storage devices, and output devices), and software engineering. Employers want to know that you've had some practical experience in design.

A growing number of schools offer courses or degrees in game design. One example is the Entertainment Technology Center (http://etc.cmu.edu) at Carnegie Mellon University. Computer programmer Shawn Patton holds a master's degree in entertainment technology from the Entertainment Technology Center (ETC). He describes the ETC as "a mixture of technologists and artists." Much of the ETC's courses involve collaborative efforts, with both students and professor providing feedback on group projects. Patton says, "The ETC grants its students the ability to experience real work with the safety net of being able to fail (and not lose your job) as long as you learn from that failure."

According to Professor Ian Parberry of the LARC, the quality of your education depends a lot on you. "You must take control of your education, seek out the best professors, and go beyond the material presented in class. What you have a right to expect from an undergraduate computer science degree is a grasp of the fundamental concepts of computer science and enough practical skills to be able to grow, learn, and thrive in any computational environment, be it computer games or otherwise."

Other Requirements

One major requirement for game design is that you must love to play computer games. You need to continually keep up with technology, which changes fast. Although you might not always use them, you need to have a variety of skills, such as writing stories, programming, and designing sound effects.

You must also have vision and the ability to identify your players and anticipate their every move in your game. You'll also have to be able to communicate well with programmers, writers, artists, musicians, electronics engineers, production workers, and others.

You must have the endurance to see a project through from beginning to end and also be able to recognize when a design should be scrapped.

Shawn Patton also advises, "An analytical mind is a must. If you like solving problems by thinking about all the variables, all the possible outcomes of your actions, and then applying those actions in a clear and concise manner, you probably have an analytical mind."

EXPLORING

One of the best ways to learn about game design is to try to develop copies of easy games, such as *Pong* and *Pac-Man,* or try to change a game that has an editor. (Games like *Klik & Play, Empire,* and *Doom* allow players to modify them to create new circumstances and settings.)

For high school students interested in finding out more about how video games and animations are produced, the DigiPen Institute of Technology (http://www.digipen.edu) offers a summer workshop.

Two-week courses are offered during July and August, providing hands-on experience and advice on courses to take in high school to prepare yourself for postsecondary training.

Writing your own stories, puzzles, and games helps develop storytelling and problem-solving skills. Magazines such as *Computer Graphics World* (http://www.cgw.com) and *Game Developer* (http://www.gdmag.com) have articles about digital video and high-end imaging and other technical and design information.

Shawn Patton recommends "tinkering in your free time: If you have a great idea for a game or an application, sit down and try to program it in whatever language you know/have at your disposal. Learning by doing is great in computer science."

EMPLOYERS

Software publishers (such as Electronic Arts and Activision) are found throughout the country, though most are located in California, New York, Washington, and Illinois. Electronic Arts is the largest independent publisher of interactive entertainment, including several development studios; the company is known worldwide. Big media companies such as Disney have also opened interactive entertainment departments. Jobs should be available at these companies as well as with online services and interactive networks, which are growing rapidly.

Some companies are involved in producing games only for video; others produce only for computers; others make games for various platforms. For example, Nintendo produces software only for video consoles; it makes different kinds of products but focuses on arcade, sports, and role-playing games. Electronic Arts runs the gamut—video, PC, and Internet—producing games in almost every genre, from sports to adventure to edutainment.

STARTING OUT

Game designers can begin earning money either independently or as an employee of a company. It is more realistic to get any creative job you can in the industry (for example, as an artist, a play tester, a programmer, or a writer) and learn as you go, developing your design skills as you work your way up to the level of designer.

Contact company websites and sites that advertise job openings, such as Game Jobs (http://www.gamejobs.com).

In addition to a professional resume, it's a good idea to have your own website, where you can showcase your demos. Make sure you

Industry Stats

- Computer and video game sales totaled $7.3 billion in 2004—an increase of nearly 50 percent since 1996.

- The computer and video game industry has released more than 7,000 titles since 1994.

- Thirty-five percent of Americans consider game play to be their most enjoyable activity.

- The average gamer plays computer games 6.8 hours per week.

- Forty-two percent of frequent gamers play online games.

- The industry has a bright future, at least according to current game players. Fifty-three percent of game players today say they will be playing as much or more in 10 years.

Source: Entertainment Software Association

have designed at least one demo or have an impressive portfolio of design ideas and documents.

Other ways to find a job in the industry include going to job fairs (such as the Game Developers Conference, http://www.gdconf.com), where you find recruiters looking for creative people to work at their companies, and checking in with online user groups, which often post jobs on the Internet.

Also consider looking for an internship to prepare for this career. Many software and entertainment companies hire interns for short-term assignments. For example, Shawn Patton completed an internship at Walt Disney Imagineering in Glendale, California, where he helped develop the game *Toontown Online* (http://www.toontown. com). Regarding his internship, Shawn says, "What I enjoyed the most about WDI was that I was able to work on code that was immediately released to the public, who then gave feedback on it. . . . I liked knowing that something I made was being used by and entertaining someone else. That's a feeling I hope to find in whatever job I end up having."

ADVANCEMENT

Just as with many jobs, to have better opportunities to advance their position and possibly earn more money, computer and video game designers have to keep up with technology. They must be willing to constantly learn more about design, the industry, and even financial and legal matters involved in development.

Becoming and remaining great at their job may be a career-long endeavor for computer and video game designers, or just a stepping-stone to another area of interactive entertainment. Some designers start out as artists, writers, or programmers, learning enough in these jobs to eventually design. For example, a person entering this career may begin as a 3-D animation modeler and work on enough game life cycles to understand what it takes to be a game designer. He or she may decide to specialize in another area, such as sound effects or even budgeting.

Some designers rise to management positions, such as president or vice president of a software publisher. Others write for magazines and books, teach, or establish their own game companies.

EARNINGS

Most development companies spend up to two years designing a game even before any of the mechanics (such as writing final code and drawing final graphics) begin; more complex games take even longer. Companies budget $1 to 3 million for developing just one game. If the game is a success, designers are often rewarded with bonuses. In addition to bonuses or royalties (the percentage of profits designers receive from each game that is sold), designers' salaries are affected by their amount of professional experience, their location in the country, and the size of their employer. Gama Network, an organization serving electronic games developers, surveyed subscribers, members, and attendees of its three divisions (*Game Developer* magazine, Gamasutra.com, and the Game Developers Conference) to find out what professionals in the game development industry were earning. Conducted in 2003, the survey reveals that game designers with one to two years' experience had an average annual salary of approximately $41,652. Those with two to five years of experience averaged $53,031 annually, and those with more than six years of experience averaged $64,249 per year. The highest reported annual salary was $300,000. It is important to note that these salaries are averages, and some designers (especially those at the beginning stages of their careers) earn less than these amounts. These figures, however, provide a useful guide for the range of earnings available.

Any major software publisher will likely provide benefits such as medical insurance, paid vacations, and retirement plans. Designers who are self-employed must provide their own benefits.

WORK ENVIRONMENT

Computer and video game designers work in office settings, whether at a large company or a home studio. At some companies, artists and designers sometimes find themselves working 24 or 48 hours at a time, so the office areas are set up with sleeping couches and other areas where employees can relax. Because the game development industry is competitive, many designers find themselves under a lot of pressure from deadlines, design problems, and budget concerns.

OUTLOOK

Computer and video games are a fast-growing segment of the U.S. entertainment industry. In fact, the NPD Group, a market information provider, reports that sales of computer and video games reached $7.3 billion in 2004. As the demand for new games, more sophisticated games, and games to be played on new systems grows, more and more companies will hire skilled people to create and perfect these products. Opportunities for game designers, therefore, should be good.

In any case, game development is popular; the Entertainment Software Association estimates that about 60 percent of the U.S. population (approximately 145 million people) play computer and video games. People in the industry expect more and more integration of interactive entertainment into mainstream society. Online development tools such as engines, graphic and sound libraries, and programming languages such as Java will probably create opportunities for new types of products that can feature game components.

FOR MORE INFORMATION

For information on associate and bachelor of science degrees in computer animation and simulation, contact
DigiPen Institute of Technology
5001 150th Avenue, NE
Redmond, WA 98052
Tel: 425-558-0299
Email: info@digipen.edu
http://www.digipen.edu

For industry information and statistics, contact
Entertainment Software Association
575 7th Street, NW, Suite 300
Washington, DC 20004

Email: esa@theesa.com
http://www.theesa.com

Visit IGDA's website for a wealth of information on careers in computer and video game design.
International Game Developers Association (IGDA)
870 Market Street, Suite 1181
San Francisco, CA 94102
Phone: 415-738-2104
Email: info@igda.org
http://www.igda.org

For information on training programs to become game designers and programmers, contact
Laboratory for Recreational Computing
University of North Texas
Department of Computer Science
PO Box 311277
Denton, TX 76203
Tel: 940-565-2681
Email: ian@cs.unt.edu
http://larc.csci.unt.edu

Computer Programmers

OVERVIEW

Computer programmers work in the field of electronic data processing. They write instructions that tell computers what to do in a computer language, or code, that the computer understands. Maintenance tasks include giving computers instructions on how to allocate time to various jobs they receive from computer terminals and making sure that these assignments are performed properly. There are approximately 499,000 computer programmers employed in the United States.

HISTORY

Data processing systems and their support personnel are a product of World War II. The amount of information that had to be compiled and organized for war efforts became so great that it was not possible for people to collect it and put it in order in time for the necessary decisions to be made. It was obvious that a quicker way had to be devised to gather and organize information if decisions based on logic and not on guesses were to be made.

After the war, the new computer technology was put to use in other government operations as well as in busi-

nesses. The first computer used in a civilian capacity was installed by the Bureau of the Census in 1951 to help compile data from the 1950 census. At this time, computers were so large, cumbersome, and energy draining that the only practical use for them was thought to be large projects such as the census. However, three years later the first computer was installed by a business firm. Since 1954, many thousands of data processing systems have been installed in government agencies, industrial firms, banks, insurance agencies, educational systems, publishing houses, colleges and universities, and scientific laboratories.

Although computers seem capable of doing just about anything, one thing is still as true of computers today as it was of the first computer 60 years ago—they cannot think for themselves. Computers are machines that can only do exactly what they are told. This requires a small army of qualified computer programmers who understand computer languages well enough to give computers instructions on what to do, when, and how in order to meet the needs of government, business, and individuals. Some programmers are currently working on artificial intelligence, or computers that can in fact "think" for themselves and make humanlike decisions, but perfection of such technology is far off. As long as there are computers and new computer applications, there will be a constant need for programmers.

THE JOB

Broadly speaking, there are two types of computer programmers. *Systems programmers* maintain the instructions, called programs or software, that control the entire computer system, including both the central processing unit and the equipment with which it communicates, such as terminals, printers, and disk drives. *Applications programmers* write the software to handle specific jobs and may specialize in engineering, scientific, or business programs. Some of the latter specialists may be designated *chief business programmers,* who supervise the work of other business programmers.

Programmers are often given program specifications prepared by *systems analysts,* who list in detail the steps the computer must follow in order to complete a given task. Programmers then code these instructions in a computer language the computer understands. In smaller companies, both analysis and programming may be handled by a *programmer/analyst.*

Before actually writing the computer program, a programmer must analyze the work request, understand the current problem and desired resolution, decide on an approach to the problem, and plan what the machine will have to do to produce the required results. Programmers prepare a flowchart to show the steps in sequence that the machine must make. They must pay attention to minute details and instruct the machine in each step of the process.

These instructions are then coded in one of several programming languages, such as BASIC, COBOL, FORTRAN, PASCAL, RPG, CSP, or C++. When the program is completed, the programmer tests its working practicality by running it on simulated data. If the machine responds according to expectations, actual data will be fed into it and the program will be activated. If the computer does not respond as anticipated, the program will have to be debugged, that is, examined for errors that must be eliminated. Finally, the programmer prepares an instruction sheet for the computer operator who will run the program.

The programmer's job concerns both an overall picture of the problem at hand and the minute detail of potential solutions. Programmers work from two points of view: from that of the people who need certain results and from that of technological problem solving. The work is divided equally between meeting the needs of other people and comprehending the capabilities of the machines.

Electronic data systems involve more than just one machine. Depending on the kind of system being used, the operation may require other machines such as printers or other peripherals. Introducing a new piece of equipment to an existing system often requires programmers to rewrite many programs.

Programmers may specialize in certain types of work, depending on the kind of problem to be solved and on the employer. Making a program for a payroll is, for example, very different from programming the study of structures of chemical compounds. Programmers who specialize in a certain field or industry generally have education or experience in that area before they are promoted to senior programming positions. *Information system programmers* specialize in programs for storing and retrieving physical science, engineering, or medical information; text analysis; and language, law, military, or library science data. As the information superhighway continues to grow, information system programmers have increased opportunities in online businesses, such as those of Lexis/Nexis, Westlaw, America Online, Microsoft, and many others.

Process control programmers develop programs for systems that control automatic operations for commercial and industrial enterprises, such as steelmaking, sanitation plants, combustion systems, computerized production testing, or automatic truck loading. *Numerical control tool programmers* program the tape that controls the machining of automatic machine tools.

REQUIREMENTS

High School
In high school you should take any computer programming or computer science courses available. You should also concentrate on math, science, and schematic drawing courses, since these subjects directly prepare students for careers in computer programming.

Postsecondary Training
Most employers prefer their programmers to be college graduates. In the past, as the field was first taking shape, employers were known to hire people with some formal education and little or no experience but determination and the ability to learn quickly. As the market becomes saturated with individuals wishing to break into this field, however, a college degree is becoming increasingly important. The U.S. Department of Labor reports that nearly half of computer programmers held a bachelor's degree or higher in 2002. One in five held a graduate degree in 2002.

Many personnel officers administer aptitude tests to determine potential for programming work. Some employers send new employees to computer schools or in-house training sessions before the employees are considered qualified to assume programming responsibilities. Training periods may last as long as a few weeks, months, or even a year.

Many junior and community colleges also offer two-year associate degree programs in data processing, computer programming, and other computer-related technologies.

Most four-year colleges and universities have computer science departments with a variety of computer-related majors, any of which could prepare a student for a career in programming. Employers who require a college degree often do not express a preference as to major field of study, although mathematics or computer science is highly favored. Other acceptable majors may be business administration, accounting, engineering, or physics. Entrance requirements for jobs with the government are much the same as those in private industry.

Certification or Licensing
Students who choose to obtain a two-year degree might consider becoming certified by the Institute for Certification of Computing Professionals, whose address is listed at the end of this article. Although it is not required, certification may boost an individual's attractiveness to employers during the job search.

Other Requirements

Personal qualifications such as a high degree of reasoning ability, patience, and persistence, as well as an aptitude for mathematics, are important for computer programmers. Some employers whose work is highly technical require that programmers be qualified in the area in which the firm or agency operates. Engineering firms, for example, prefer young people with an engineering background and are willing to train them in some programming techniques. For other firms, such as banks, consumer-level knowledge of the services that banks offer may be sufficient background for incoming programmers.

EXPLORING

If you are interested in becoming a computer programmer, you might visit a large bank or insurance company in the community and seek an appointment to talk with one of the programmers on the staff. You may be able to visit the data processing center and see the machines in operation. You might also talk with a sales representative from one of the large manufacturers of data processing equipment and request whatever brochures or pamphlets the company publishes.

It is a good idea to start early and get some hands-on experience operating and programming a computer. A trip to the local library or bookstore is likely to turn up countless books on programming; this is one field where the resources to teach yourself are highly accessible and available for all levels of competency. Joining a computer club and reading professional magazines are other ways to become more familiar with this career field. In addition, you should start exploring the Internet, itself a great source of information about computer-related careers.

High school and college students who can operate a computer may be able to obtain part-time jobs in business computer centers or in some larger companies. Any computer experience will be helpful for future computer training.

EMPLOYERS

There are approximately 499,000 computer programming jobs in the United States, and programmers work in locations across the country and in almost every type of business. They work for manufacturing companies, data processing service firms, hardware and software companies, banks, insurance companies, credit companies, publishing houses, government agencies, and colleges and universities throughout the country. Many programmers are employed by businesses as consultants on a temporary or contractual basis.

STARTING OUT

You can look for an entry-level programming position in the same way as most other jobs; there is no special or standard point of entry into the field. Individuals with the necessary qualifications should apply directly to companies, agencies, or industries that have announced job openings through a school placement office, an employment agency, or the classified ads.

Students in two- or four-year degree programs should work closely with their schools' career services offices, since major local employers often list job openings exclusively with such offices.

If the market for programmers is particularly tight, you may want to obtain an entry-level job with a large corporation or computer software firm, even if the job does not include programming. As jobs in the programming department open up, current employees in other departments are often the first to know, and they are favored over nonemployees during the interviewing process. Getting a foot in the door in this way has proven to be successful for many programmers.

ADVANCEMENT

Programmers are ranked as junior or senior programmers, according to education, experience, and level of responsibility. After programmers have attained the highest available programming position, they can choose to make one of several career moves in order to be promoted still higher.

Some programmers are more interested in the analysis aspect of computing than in the actual charting and coding of programming. They often acquire additional training and experience in order to prepare themselves for promotion to positions as systems programmers or systems analysts. These individuals have the added responsibility of working with upper management to define equipment and cost guidelines for a specific project. They perform only broad programming tasks, leaving most of the detail work to programmers.

Other programmers become more interested in administration and management and may wish to become heads of programming departments. They tend to be more people oriented and enjoy leading others to excellence. As the level of management responsibilities increases, the amount of technical work performed decreases, so management positions are not for everyone.

Still other programmers may branch out into different technical areas, such as total computer operations, hardware design, and software or network engineering. With experience, they may be placed in charge of the data systems center. They may also decide to go to work for a consulting company, work that generally pays extremely well.

Programming provides a solid background in the computer industry. Experienced programmers enjoy a wide variety of possibilities for career advancement. The hardest part for programmers usually is deciding exactly what they want to do.

EARNINGS

According to the National Association of Colleges and Employers, the starting annual salary for college graduates with computer programming bachelor's degrees averaged $45,558 in 2003. The U.S. Department of Labor reports the median annual salary for computer programmers was $62,980 in 2004. The lowest paid 10 percent of programmers earned less than $37,170 annually, and at the other end of the pay scale, the highest paid 10 percent earned more than $100,980 that same year. Programmers in the West and the Northeast are generally paid more than those in the South and Midwest. This is because most big computer companies are located in the Silicon Valley in California or in the state of Washington, where Microsoft, a major employer of programmers, has its headquarters. Also, some industries, such as public utilities and data processing service firms, tend to pay their programmers higher wages than do other types of employers, such as banks and schools.

Most programmers receive the customary paid vacation and sick leave and are included in such company benefits as group insurance and retirement benefit plans.

WORK ENVIRONMENT

Most programmers work in pleasant office conditions, since computers require an air-conditioned, dust-free environment. Programmers perform most of their duties in one primary location but may be asked to travel to other computing sites on occasion. Because of advances in technology, telecommuting is an increasingly common option for computer professionals, allowing them to work remotely.

The average programmer works between 35 and 40 hours weekly. In some job situations, the programmer may have to work nights or weekends on short notice. This might happen when a program is going through its trial runs, for example, or when there are many demands for additional services. As with other workers who spend long periods in front of a computer terminal typing at a keyboard, programmers are susceptible to eyestrain, back discomfort, and hand and wrist problems, such as carpal tunnel syndrome.

OUTLOOK

The employment rate for computer programmers is expected to increase about as fast as the average through 2012, according to the U.S. Department of Labor. Employment of programmers is expected to grow more slowly than that of other computer specialists. Factors that make job growth for this profession slower than job growth for other computer industry professions include new technologies that eliminate the need for some routine programming work of the past, the increased availability of packaged software programs, and the increased sophistication of computer users who are able to write and implement their own programs. Jobs should be most plentiful in data processing service firms, software houses, and computer consulting businesses.

Job applicants with the best chances of employment will be college graduates with a knowledge of several programming languages, especially newer ones used for computer networking and database management. In addition, the best applicants will have some training or experience in an applied field such as accounting, science, engineering, or management. Competition for jobs will be heavier among graduates of two-year data processing programs and among people with equivalent experience or with less training. Since this field is constantly changing, programmers should stay abreast of the latest technology to remain competitive. Growing emphasis on cyber-security will lead to demand for programmers familiar with digital security issues.

FOR MORE INFORMATION

For more information about careers in computer programming, contact the following organizations:
Association for Computing Machinery
1515 Broadway
New York, NY 10036
Tel: 800-342-6626
Email: sigs@acm.org
http://www.acm.org

Association of Information Technology Professionals
401 North Michigan Avenue, Suite 2400
Chicago, IL 60611-4267
Tel: 800-224-9371
http://www.aitp.org

Institute of Electrical and Electronics Engineers Computer Society
1730 Massachusetts Avenue, NW
Washington, DC 20036-1992
Tel: 202-371-0101
http://www.computer.org

National Workforce Center for Emerging Technologies
Bellevue Community College
3000 Landerholm Circle, SE, N258
Bellevue, WA 98007-6484
http://www.nwcet.org

For information on certification programs, contact
Institute for Certification of Computing Professionals
2350 East Devon Avenue, Suite 115
Des Plaines, IL 60018-4610
Tel: 800-843-8227
Email: office@iccp.org
http://www.iccp.org

Computer Science Professors

QUICK FACTS

School Subjects
Computers
English
Speech

Personal Skills
Communication/ideas
Helping/teaching

Work Environment
Primarily indoors
Primarily one location

Minimum Education Level
Master's degree

Salary Range
$29,520 to $53,520 to
$95,920

Certification or Licensing
None available

Outlook
Much faster than the average

DOT
090

GOE
12.03.02

NOC
4121

O*NET-SOC
25-1021.00

OVERVIEW

Computer science professors instruct undergraduate and graduate students in the subject of computer science at colleges and universities. They are responsible for lecturing classes, leading small seminar groups, and creating and grading examinations. They also may conduct research, write for publication, and aid in administration. There are approximately 37,260 computer science teachers at the postsecondary level.

HISTORY

The concept of colleges and universities goes back many centuries. These institutions evolved slowly from monastery schools, which trained a select few for certain professions, notably theology. The terms *college* and *university* have become virtually interchangeable in America outside the walls of academia, although originally they designated two very different kinds of institutions.

Two of the most notable early European universities were the University of Bologna in Italy, thought to have been established in the 12th century, and the University of Paris, which was chartered in 1201. These universities were considered to be models after which other European universities were patterned. Oxford University in England was probably established during the 12th century. Oxford served as a model for early American colleges and universities and today is still considered one of the world's leading institutions.

26

Harvard, the first U.S. college, was established in 1636. Its stated purpose was to train men for the ministry; the early colleges were all established for religious training. With the growth of state-supported institutions in the early 18th century, the process of freeing the curriculum from ties with the church began. The University of Virginia established the first liberal arts curriculum in 1825, and these innovations were later adopted by many other colleges and universities.

Although the original colleges in the United States were patterned after Oxford University, they later came under the influence of German universities. During the 19th century, more than 9,000 Americans went to Germany to study. The emphasis in German universities was on the scientific method. Most of the people who had studied in Germany returned to the United States to teach in universities, bringing this objective, factual approach to education and to other fields of learning.

In 1833, Oberlin College in Oberlin, Ohio, became the first college founded as a coeducational institution. In 1836, the first women-only college, Wesleyan Female College, was founded in Macon, Georgia.

The junior college movement in the United States has been one of the most rapidly growing educational developments. Junior colleges first came into being just after the turn of the 20th century.

The first computer science program was founded at Harvard University. Today, nearly every college and university in the United States offers computer science or information technology–related majors.

THE JOB

Computer science faculty members teach at junior colleges or at four-year colleges and universities. At four-year institutions, most faculty members are *assistant professors, associate professors,* or *full professors.* These three types of professorships differ in regards to status, job responsibilities, and salary. Assistant professors are new faculty members who are working to get tenure (status as a permanent professor); they seek to advance to associate and then to full professorships.

Computer science professors perform three main functions: teaching, advising, and research. Their most important responsibility is to teach students. Their role within the department will determine the level of courses they teach and the number of courses per semester. Most professors work with students at all levels, from college freshmen to graduate students. They may head several classes a semester or only a few a year. Some of their classes will have large enrollment, while graduate seminars may consist of only 12 or fewer students. Though professors may spend fewer than 10 hours a week in the actual classroom, they spend many hours preparing lectures and lesson plans, grading papers and exams, and preparing grade reports. They also schedule office hours during the week to be available to students outside of the lecture hall, and they meet with students individually throughout the semester. In the classroom, professors lecture, lead discussions, administer exams, and assign textbook reading and other research. While most professors teach entry-level computer science classes such as "Introduction to Computer Science" or "Foundations of Computer Science," some also teach higher-level classes that centers on a particular specialty. For a computer graphics class, for example, professors may teach students how to create computerized animation, digital illustration, or Web design. Professors teaching software engineering classes may specialize in software design and development or information systems. In some courses, they rely heavily on computer laboratories to teach course material.

Another important responsibility is advising students. Not all faculty members serve as advisers, but those who do must set aside large blocks of time to guide students through the program. College professors who serve as advisers may have any number of students assigned to them, from fewer than 10 to more than 100, depending on the administrative policies of the college. Their responsibility may involve looking over a planned program of studies to make sure the students meet requirements for graduation, or it may involve working intensively with each student on many aspects of college life. They may also discuss the different fields of computer science with students and help them identify the best career choices.

The third responsibility of college and university faculty members is research and publication. Faculty members who are heavily involved in research programs sometimes are assigned a smaller teaching load. College professors publish their research findings in various scholarly journals. They also write books based on their research or on their own knowledge and experience in the field. Most textbooks are written by college and university teachers, or veterans of the computer industry.

Publishing a significant amount of work has been the traditional standard by which assistant professors prove themselves worthy of becoming permanent, tenured faculty. Typically, pressure to publish is greatest for assistant professors. Pressure to publish increases again if an associate professor wishes to be considered for a promotion to full professorship.

In recent years, some liberal arts colleges have recognized that the pressure to publish is taking faculty away from their primary duties to the students, and these institutions have begun to place a decreasing emphasis on publishing and more on performance in the classroom. Professors in junior colleges face less pressure to publish than those in four-year institutions.

Some faculty members eventually rise to the position of *department chair,* where they govern the affairs of an entire computer science department. Department chairs, faculty, and other professional staff members are aided in their myriad duties by *graduate assistants,* who may help develop teaching materials, moderate computer laboratories, conduct research, give examinations, teach introductory courses, and carry out other activities.

Some computer science professors may also conduct classes in an extension program. In such a program, they teach evening and weekend courses for the benefit of people who otherwise would not be able to take advantage of the institution's resources. They may travel away from the campus and meet with a group of students at another location. They may work full time for the extension division or may divide their time between on-campus and off-campus teaching.

Distance learning programs, an increasingly popular option for students, give professors the opportunity to use today's technologies to remain in one place while teaching students who are at a variety of locations simultaneously. The professor's duties, like those when teaching correspondence courses conducted by mail, include grading work that students send in at periodic intervals and advising students of their progress. Computers, the Internet, email, and video conferencing, however, are some of the technology tools that allow professors and students to communicate in "real time" in a virtual classroom setting. Meetings may be scheduled during the same time as traditional classes or during evenings and weekends. Professors who do this work are sometimes known as *extension work, correspondence,* or *distance learning instructors.* They may teach online courses in addition to other classes or may have distance learning as their major teaching responsibility.

The *junior college instructor* has many of the same kinds of responsibilities as does the teacher in a four-year college or university. Because junior colleges offer only a two-year program, they teach only undergraduates.

Students listen attentively as a computer science professor outlines a key concept. *(Corbis)*

REQUIREMENTS

High School

Your high school's college preparatory program likely includes courses in computers (as many as you can take), English, science, foreign language, history, and mathematics. In addition, you should take courses in speech to get a sense of what it will be like to lecture to a group of students. Your school's debate team can also help you develop public speaking skills, along with research skills.

Postsecondary Training

At least one advanced degree in your field of study is required to be a professor in a college or university. The master's degree is considered the minimum standard, and graduate work beyond the master's is usually desirable. If you hope to advance in academic rank above instructor, most institutions require a doctorate. Many large universities and colleges have a strong preference to those with a Ph.D. in computer science, information management, or a closely related field.

In the last year of your undergraduate program, you'll apply to graduate programs in your area of study. Standards for admission to a graduate program can be high and the competition heavy, depending on the school. Once accepted into a program, your responsibilities will be similar to those of your professors—in addition to attending seminars, you'll research, prepare articles for publication, and teach some undergraduate courses.

You may find employment in a junior college with only a master's degree. Advancement in responsibility and in salary, however, is more likely to come if you have earned a doctorate.

Other Requirements

You should definitely like working with computers, but also enjoy reading, writing, and researching. Not only will you spend many years studying in school, but your whole career will be based on communicating your thoughts and ideas, as well as abstract concepts to students. People skills are important because you'll be dealing directly with students, administrators, and other faculty members on a daily basis. You should feel comfortable in a role of authority and possess self-confidence.

EXPLORING

Learn as much as you can about computer hardware, computer software, and the Internet. Visit websites and read books and magazines that relate to computers.

Your high school computer science teachers use many of the same skills as college computer science professors, so talk to your teachers about their careers and their college experiences. You can develop your own teaching experience by volunteering at a community center, working at a day care center, or working at a summer camp. Also, spend some time on a college campus to get a sense of the environment. Write to colleges for their admissions brochures and course catalogs (or check them out online); read about the faculty members and the courses they teach. Before visiting college campuses, make arrangements to speak to professors who teach courses that interest you. These professors may allow you to sit in on their classes or labs and observe. Also, make appointments with college advisers and with people in the admissions and recruitment offices. If your grades are good enough, you might be able to serve as a teaching assistant during your undergraduate years, which can give you experience leading discussions and grading papers.

EMPLOYERS

Approximately 37,260 computer science faculty are employed in the United States. Employment opportunities vary based on area of study and education. Most universities have many different departments that hire faculty. With a doctorate, a number of publications, and a record of good teaching, professors should find opportunities in universities all across the country. There are more than 3,800 colleges and universities in the United States. Professors teach in undergraduate and graduate programs. The teaching jobs at doctoral institutions are usually better paying and more prestigious. The most sought-after positions are those that offer tenure. Teachers who have only a master's degree will be limited to opportunities with junior colleges, community colleges, and some small private institutions.

STARTING OUT

You should start the process of finding a teaching position while you are in graduate school. The process includes developing a curriculum vitae (a detailed, academic resume), writing for publication, assisting with research, attending conferences, and gaining teaching experience and recommendations. Many students begin applying for teaching positions while finishing their graduate program. For most positions at four-year institutions, you must travel to large conferences where interviews can be arranged with representatives from the universities to which you have applied.

Because of the competition for tenure-track positions, you may have to work for a few years in temporary positions, visiting various schools as an *adjunct professor*. Some professional associations maintain lists of teaching opportunities in their areas. They may also make lists of applicants available to college administrators looking to fill an available position.

Some professors begin teaching after having successful careers in the computer industry.

ADVANCEMENT

The normal pattern of advancement is from instructor to assistant professor, to associate professor, to full professor. All four academic ranks are concerned primarily with teaching and research. College faculty members who have an interest in and a talent for administration may be advanced to department chair or dean of their college. A few become college or university presidents or other types of administrators.

The instructor is usually an inexperienced college teacher. He or she may hold a doctorate or may have completed all the Ph.D. requirements except for the dissertation. Most colleges look upon the rank of instructor as the period during which the college is trying out the teacher. Instructors usually are advanced to the position of assistant professors within three to four years. Assistant professors are given up to about six years to prove themselves worthy of tenure, and if they do so, they become associate professors. Some professors choose to remain at the associate level. Others strive to become full professors and receive greater status, salary, and responsibilities.

Most colleges have clearly defined promotion policies from rank to rank for faculty members, and many have written statements about the number of years in which instructors and assistant professors may remain in grade. Administrators in many colleges hope to encourage younger faculty members to increase their skills and competencies and thus to qualify for the more responsible positions of associate professor and full professor.

EARNINGS

According to the U.S. Department of Labor, in 2004 the median salary for all computer science postsecondary instructors was $53,520, with 10 percent earning $95,920 or more and 10 percent earning $29,520 or less. Those with the highest earnings tend to be senior tenured faculty; those with the lowest, graduate assistants. Professors working on the West Coast and the East Coast and those working at doctorate-granting institutions also tend to have the highest salaries. Many professors try to increase their earnings by completing research, publishing in their field, or teaching additional courses.

Benefits for full-time faculty typically include health insurance and retirement funds and, in some cases, stipends for travel related to research, housing allowances, and tuition waivers for dependents.

WORK ENVIRONMENT

A college or university is usually a pleasant place in which to work. Campuses bustle with all types of activities and events, stimulating ideas, and a young, energetic population. Much prestige comes with success as a professor and scholar; professors have the respect of students, colleagues, and others in their community.

Depending on the size of the department, computer science professors may have their own office, or they may have to share an office with one or more colleagues. Their department may provide them with a computer, Internet access, and research assistants. College professors are also able to do much of their office work at home. They can arrange their schedule around class hours, academic meetings, and the established office hours when they meet with students. Most computer science teachers work more than 40 hours each week. Although computer science teachers may teach only two or three classes a semester, they spend many hours preparing for lectures, examining student work, and conducting research.

OUTLOOK

The U.S. Department of Labor predicts much faster than average employment growth for college and university professors through 2012. College enrollment is projected to grow due to an increased number of 18- to 24-year-olds, an increased number of adults returning to college, and an increased number of foreign-born students. Retirement of current faculty members will also provide job openings. However, competition for full-time, tenure-track positions at four-year schools will be very strong.

FOR MORE INFORMATION

To read about the issues affecting college professors, contact the following organizations:

American Association of University Professors
1012 14th Street, NW, Suite 500
Washington, DC 20005
Tel: 202-737-5900
Email: aaup@aaup.org
http://www.aaup.org

American Federation of Teachers
555 New Jersey Avenue, NW
Washington, DC 20001
Tel: 202-879-4400
Email: online@aft.org
http://www.aft.org

Computer Systems Programmer/Analysts

OVERVIEW

Computer systems programmer/analysts analyze the computing needs of a business and then design a new system or upgrade an old system to meet those needs. The position can be split between two people, the *systems programmer* and the *systems analyst,* but it is frequently held by just one person, who oversees the work from beginning to end. Approximately 468,000 computer systems programmer/analysts are employed in the United States.

HISTORY

The first major advances in modern computer technology were made during World War II. After the war, people thought that computers were too big (they easily filled entire warehouses) to ever be used for anything other than government projects, such as the processing of the 1950 census.

The introduction of semiconductors to computer technology led to the creation of smaller and less expensive computers. The semiconductors replaced the bigger, slower vacuum tubes of the first computers. These changes made it easier for businesses to adapt computers to their needs, which they began doing as early as 1954. Within 30 years, computers had revolutionized the way people work, play, and even shop. Today, computers are everywhere, from businesses of all kinds to government agencies, charitable organizations, and private homes. Over the years, technology has continued to shrink computer size and increase operating speeds at an unprecedented rate.

The need for systems programmer/analysts grew out of the proliferation of hardware and software products on the market. While many offices have an unofficial "computer expert," whose main job may be in accounting, word processing, or office administration, most medium-size to larger companies that have invested in expensive computer systems have found the need to employ, either full time or on a consulting basis, a systems analyst or programmer/analyst.

In addition, the computer revolution brought with it awareness that choosing the appropriate system from the start is crucial to business success. Purchasing decisions are based on many complicated scientific and mathematical models as well as on practical business sense. Therefore, systems analysts have become essential to business decision-making.

Businesses and organizations also discovered that, like all new technology, computer systems break down a lot. It has become more cost effective for many organizations to have full-time systems analysts on site instead of calling computer repairers to fix every small glitch.

THE JOB

Businesses invest hundreds of thousands of dollars in computer systems to make their operations more efficient and more profitable. As older systems become obsolete, businesses are also faced with the task of replacing them or upgrading them with new technology. Computer systems programmer/analysts plan and develop new computer systems or upgrade existing systems to meet changing business needs. They also install, modify, and maintain functioning computer systems. The process of choosing and implementing a computer system is similar for programmer/analysts who work for very different employers. However, specific decisions in terms of hardware and software differ depending on the industry.

The first stage of the process involves meeting with management and users in order to discuss the problem at hand. For example, a company's accounting system might be slow, unreliable, and generally outdated. During many hours of meetings, systems programmer/analysts and management discuss various options, including commercial software, hardware upgrades, and customizing possibilities that may solve the problems. At the end of the discussions, which may last as long as several weeks or months, the programmer analyst defines the specific system goals as agreed upon by participants.

Next, systems programmer/analysts engage in highly analytic and logical activities. They use tools such as structural analysis, data modeling, mathematics, and cost accounting to determine which computers, including hardware and software and peripherals, will be required to meet the goals of the project. They must consider the trade-offs between extra efficiency and speed and increased costs. Weighing the pros and cons of each additional system feature is an important factor in system planning. Whatever preliminary decisions are made must be supported by mathematical and financial evidence.

As the final stage of the planning process, systems programmer/analysts prepare reports and formal presentations to be delivered to management. Reports must be written in clear, concise language that business professionals, who are not necessarily technical experts, can understand thoroughly. Formal presentations in front of groups of various sizes are often required as part of the system proposal.

If the system or the system upgrades are approved, equipment is purchased and installed. Then, the programmer/analysts get down to the real technical work so that all the different computers and peripherals function well together. They prepare specifications, diagrams, and other programming structures and, often using computer-aided systems engineering (CASE) technology, they write the new or upgraded programming code. If they work solely as systems analysts, it is at this point that they hand over all of their information to the systems programmer so that he or she can begin to write the programming code.

Systems design and programming involves defining the files and records to be accessed by the system, outlining the processing steps, and suggesting formats for output that meet the needs of the company. User-friendliness of the front-end applications is extremely important for user productivity. Therefore, programmer/analysts must be able to envision how nontechnical system users view their on-screen work. Systems programmer/analysts might also specify security programs that allow only authorized personnel access to certain files or groups of files.

As the programs are written, programmer/analysts set up test runs of various parts of the system, making sure each step of the way that major goals are reached. Once the system is up and running, problems, or "bugs," begin to pop up. Programmer/analysts are responsible for fixing these last-minute problems. They must isolate the problem and review the hundreds of lines of programming commands to determine where the mistake is located. Then they must enter the correct command or code and recheck the program.

Depending on the employer, some systems programmer/analysts might be involved with computer networking. Network communication programs tell two or more computers or peripherals how to work with each other. When a system is composed of equipment from various manufacturers, networking is essential for smooth system functioning. For example, shared printers have to know how

Useful Books

Allen, Huey, and Joanne C. Wachter. *Careers in the Computer Field.* Success Without College Series. Hauppauge, N.J.: Barron's Educational Series, 2000.

Berners-Lee, Tim. *Weaving the Web: The Original Design and Ultimate Destiny of the World Wide Web.* New York: HarperBusiness, 2000.

Ceruzzi, Paul E. *A History of Modern Computing.* 2d ed. Cambridge, Mass.: MIT Press, 2003.

Freedman, Alan. *Computer Glossary: The Complete Illustrated Dictionary.* 9th ed. New York: American Management Association, 2000.

Gardner, Garth. *Careers in Computer Graphics & Animation.* Washington, D.C.: Garth Gardner Company, 2001.

Ifrah, Georges. *The Universal History of Computing: From the Abacus to the Quantum Computer.* Hoboken, N.J.: Wiley, 2002.

Pasternak, Ceel, and Linda Thornburg. *Cool Careers for Girls in Computers.* Manassas Park, Va.: Impact Publications, 1999.

Resumes for Computer Careers. 2d ed. New York: McGraw-Hill, 2002.

Stair, Lila B., and Leslie Stair. *Careers in Computers.* 3d ed. New York: McGraw-Hill, 2002.

to order print jobs as they come in from various terminals. Some programmer/analysts write the code that establishes printing queues. Others might be involved in user training, since they know the software applications well. They might also customize commercial software programs to meet the needs of their company.

Many programmer/analysts become specialized in an area of business, science, or engineering. They seek education and further on-the-job training in these areas to develop expertise. They may therefore attend special seminars, workshops, and classes designed for their needs. This extra knowledge allows them to develop a deeper understanding of the computing problems specific to the business or industry.

REQUIREMENTS

High School

Take a college preparatory program with advanced classes in math, science, and computer science to prepare you for this work. This will provide a foundation of basic concepts and encourage the development of analytic and logical thinking skills. Since programmer/analysts do a lot of proposal writing that may or may not be technical in nature, English classes are valuable as well. Speech classes will help prepare you for making formal presentations to management and clients.

Postsecondary Training

A bachelor's degree in computer science is a minimum requirement for systems programmer/analysts. Course work in preparation for this field includes math, computer programming, science, and logic. Several years of related work experience, including knowledge of programming languages, are often necessary as well. For some very high-level positions, an advanced degree in a specific computer subfield may be required. Also, depending on the employer, proficiency in business, science, or engineering may be necessary.

Certification or Licensing

Some programmer/analysts pursue certification through the Institute for Certification of Computing Professionals. In particular, they take classes and exams to become certified computing professionals (CCPs). Certification is voluntary and is an added credential for job hunters. CCPs have achieved a recognized level of knowledge and experience in principles and practices related to systems.

Other Requirements

Successful systems programmer/analysts demonstrate strong analytic skills and enjoy the challenges of problem solving. They are able to understand problems that exist on many levels, from technical problems to business-oriented problems. They can visualize complicated and abstract relationships between computer hardware and software and are good at matching needs to equipment.

Systems programmer/analysts have to be flexible as well. They routinely deal with many different kinds of people, from management to data entry clerks. Therefore, they must be knowledgeable in a lot of functional areas of the company. They should be able to talk to management about cost-effective solutions, to programmers about detailed coding, and to clerks about user-friendliness of the applications.

As is true for all computer professionals, systems programmer/analysts must be able to learn about new technology quickly. They should be naturally curious about keeping up on cutting-edge developments, which can be time consuming. Furthermore, they are often so busy at their jobs that staying in the know is done largely on their own time.

EXPLORING

If you are interested in this career, you have several options to learn more about what it is like to be a computer systems programmer/analyst. You can spend a day with a working professional in this field in order to experience a typical day firsthand. Career days of this type can usually be arranged through school guidance counselors or the public relations managers of local corporations.

Strategy games, such as chess, played with friends or school clubs are a good way to put your analytic thinking skills to use while having fun. When choosing a game, the key is to make sure it relies on qualities similar to those that programmer/analysts use.

Lastly, you should become a computer hobbyist and learn everything you can about computers by working and playing with them on a daily basis. Surfing the Internet regularly, as well as reading trade magazines, will also be helpful. You might also want to try hooking up a mini-system at home or school, configuring terminals, printers, modems, and other peripherals into a coherent system. This activity requires a fair amount of knowledge and should be supervised by a professional.

EMPLOYERS

There are approximately 468,000 computer systems programmer/analysts employed in the United States. Computer systems programmer/analysts work for all types of firms and organizations that do their work on computers. Such companies may include manufacturing companies, data processing service firms, hardware and software companies, banks, insurance companies, credit companies, publishing houses, government agencies, and colleges and universities. Many programmer/analysts are employed by businesses as consultants on a temporary or contractual basis.

STARTING OUT

Since systems programmer/analysts typically have at least some experience in a computer-related job, most are hired into these jobs from lower-level positions within the same company. For example, programmers, software engineering technicians, and network and database administrators all gain valuable computing experience that can be put to good use at a systems job. Alternatively, individuals who acquire expertise in systems programming and analysis while in other jobs may want to work with a headhunter to find the right systems positions for them. Also, trade magazines, newspapers, and employment agencies regularly feature job openings in this field.

Students in four-year degree programs should work closely with their schools' career services offices. Companies regularly work through such offices in order to find the most qualified graduates. Since it may be difficult to find a job as a programmer/analyst to begin with, it is important for students to consider their long-term potential within a certain company. The chance for promotion into a systems job can make lower-level jobs more appealing, at least in the short run.

For those individuals already employed in a computer-related job but wanting to get into systems programming and analysis, additional formal education is a good idea. Some employers have educational reimbursement policies that allow employees to take courses inexpensively. If the employee's training could directly benefit the business, companies are more willing to pay for the expense.

ADVANCEMENT

Systems programmer/analysts already occupy a relatively high-level technical job. Promotion, therefore, usually occurs in one of two directions. First, programmer/analysts can be put in charge of increasingly larger and more complex systems. Instead of concentrating on a company's local system, for example, an analyst can oversee all company systems and networks. This kind of technically based promotion can also put systems programmer/analysts into other areas of computing. With the proper experience and additional training, they can get into database or network management and design, software engineering, or even quality assurance.

The other direction in which programmer/analysts can go is into management. Depending on the position sought, formal education (either a bachelor's degree in business or a master's in business administration) may be required. As more administrative duties are added, more technical ones are taken away. Therefore, programmer/analysts who enjoy the technical aspect of their work more than anything else may not want to pursue this advancement track. Excellent computing managers have both a solid background in various forms of computing and a good grasp of what it takes to run a department. Also, having the vision to see how technology will change in the short and long terms, and how those changes will affect the industry concerned, is a quality of a good manager.

EARNINGS

According to the U.S. Department of Labor, the median annual salary for computer systems analysts was $67,520 in 2004. At the low end of the pay range, 10 percent of systems analysts earned less than $42,780. The top 10 percent earned more than $100,440. Salaries are slightly higher in geographic areas where many computer companies are clustered, such as Silicon Valley in California and Seattle, Washington.

Level of education also affects analysts' earnings. The National Association of Colleges and Employers reports that starting salaries for those with master's degrees in computer science averaged $62,806 in 2003. Those with bachelor's degrees in computer science, however, had starting salaries averaging $47,109, and those with bachelor's degrees in computer systems analysis averaged $41,118, also in 2003.

Those in senior positions can earn much higher salaries. *Computerworld* reports that senior systems programmers earned a national average of $71,475 in 2003, while senior systems analysts earned $76,173.

Most programmer/analysts receive health insurance, paid vacation, and sick leave. Some employers offer tuition reimbursement programs and in-house computer training workshops.

WORK ENVIRONMENT

Computer systems programmer/analysts work in comfortable office environments. If they work as consultants, they may travel frequently. Otherwise, travel is limited to trade shows, seminars, and visitations to vendors for demonstrations. They might also visit other businesses to observe their systems in action.

Programmer/analysts usually work 40-hour weeks and enjoy the regular holiday schedule of days off. However, as deadlines for system installation, upgrades, and spot-checking approach, they are often required to work overtime. Extra compensation for overtime hours may come in the form of time-and-a-half pay or compensatory time off, depending on the precise nature of the employee's duties, company policy, and state law. If the employer operates off-shifts, programmer/analysts may be on-call to address any problems that might arise at any time of the day or night. This is relatively rare in the service sector but more common in manufacturing, heavy industry, and data processing firms.

Computer systems programming and analysis is very detailed work. The smallest error can cause major system disruptions, which can be a great source of frustration. Systems programmer/analysts must be prepared to deal with this frustration and be able to work well under pressure.

OUTLOOK

The U.S. Department of Labor predicts that the job of computer systems programmer/analyst will be one of the fastest growing careers through 2012, with employment increasing much faster than the average. Increases are mainly a product of the growing number of businesses that rely extensively on computers. When businesses automate, their daily operations depend on the capacity of their computer systems to perform at desired levels. The continuous development of new technologies means that businesses must also update their old systems to remain competitive in the marketplace. Additionally, the need for businesses to network their information adds to the demand for qualified programmer/analysts. Businesses will rely increasingly on systems programmer/analysts to make the right purchasing decisions and to keep systems running smoothly.

Many computer manufacturers are beginning to expand the range of services they offer to business clients. In the years to come, they may hire many systems programmer/analysts to work as consultants on a per-project basis with a potential client. These workers would perform essentially the same duties, with the addition of extensive follow-up maintenance. They would analyze business needs and suggest proper systems to answer them. In addition, more and more independent consulting firms are hiring systems programmer/analysts to perform the same tasks.

Analysts with advanced degrees in computer science, management information systems, or computer engineering will be in great demand. Individuals with master's degrees in business administration with emphasis in information systems will also be highly desirable.

FOR MORE INFORMATION

For more information about systems programmer/analyst positions, contact

Association of Information Technology Professionals
401 North Michigan Avenue, Suite 2400
Chicago, IL 60611-4267
Tel: 800-224-9371
http://www.aitp.org

For information on becoming an independent consultant, contact
Independent Computer Consultants Association
11131 South Towne Square, Suite F
St. Louis, MO 63123
Tel: 800-774-4222
Email: info@icca.org
http://www.icca.org

For information on certification programs, contact
Institute for Certification of Computing Professionals
2350 East Devon Avenue, Suite 115
Des Plaines, IL 60018-4610
Tel: 800-843-8227
Email: office@iccp.org
http://www.iccp.org

Digital Agents

OVERVIEW

Digital agents represent people who have excellent technology skills and knowledge and market these talents to companies that are in need of technical expertise. They may represent both people who want to work on a project-by-project basis or those who are looking for full-time salaried positions. Companies also come to digital agents seeking their help in finding employees with appropriate technology skills. Digital agents must have excellent technical knowledge to match people and companies.

HISTORY

As the Internet has grown in leaps and bounds over the past decade, the computer industry professionals responsible for innovations in Internet and computer technology became highly sought after by private companies and government agencies. Their expertise often translated into huge profits and steady performance for companies and other organizations wise enough to hire the best workers. As demand grew for their services, agents began to represent computer professionals—locating the most lucrative and rewarding positions for their clients. These agents eventually became known as digital agents. Although the digital agent's job is relatively new, the expanding use of increasingly complex computers and the Internet in the workplace may mean that this profession should become quite important in the coming decades.

THE JOB

Digital agents work exclusively within the high-tech world. They are responsible for finding their clients suitable work and are also responsible to the companies that come to their agencies looking for appropriate help. An agent may work with clients who are independent contractors (freelancers who work on a project for one company, then work on another project for a different company) or with clients who are looking for full-time salaried positions. No matter what type of employment the client wants, however, the agent will spend considerable time getting to know his or her skills and goals. Only agents who understand their clients will be able to find them the best positions.

Bill Hughes, a digital agent for Aquent, a national, high-tech talent agency, explains, "I primarily represent the most talented people in the high tech/computer field that I can find. I represent them exclusively and find them a contract or permanent job."

The digital agent's job, though, is not the same as that of a traditional job recruiter or placement executive. "I don't have to place my people in order to get paid," Hughes emphasizes. "The typical recruiter gets paid a straight commission based on how many people he can place on a job." Recruiters who work on commission, Hughes feels, often push employees into taking jobs at companies even though it may not be a good match. "Because I am paid salary and no commissions, I can afford to spend time with my talent and the prospective companies who are looking for these specialized people." In this way, Hughes can make matches that will make both the client and the company happy.

The digital agent interviews new clients, or talents, to find out what their skills are and what type of work they would like to have. What kind of software is the client comfortable using? Does the client enjoy doing Web design? What is the client's education and previous work experience? Does the client want to work freelance or as a salaried employee of a company? "I take the time to know my talent and their career paths," Hughes says.

The agent also needs to interview representatives of companies who are looking for employees. Does the company want someone to do Web design, strategic planning for e-commerce, or some other job? What computer skills do they feel the employee should have? How long will the project last? Will the employee be working as a member of a team or independently? Agents will ask as many questions as they need to get a feel for the company's requirements so that a good match can be made. Good communication skills are essential for agents. Hughes says, "I also take the time to listen to the companies and understand the type of skills they are looking for."

While Hughes works mostly with individuals who have specific computer-related skills, some digital agents represent small firms or groups of talented high-tech workers. Frequently these small firms do specialized work, and they are sometimes known as "boutique firms." Digital agents match these small firms with other companies that need their unique services.

Because the Web industry is so fragmented and rapidly growing, it can be difficult for small firms to get the visibility they need in the field in order to establish themselves. Digital agents representing these small firms can make the firms' services known to large corporations in need of technical help. Again, the agent will have interviewed members of the small firm so that he or she knows the firm's area of expertise. The agent will also know what type of larger company the firm may want to work with. Then, through the agency's connections, the digital agent will contact larger companies or establishments that are in need of such services. The agent must also keep budgets in mind when doing this work, since what the larger company is willing to pay for the work must match with what the small firm is willing to accept.

Digital agents must be computer savvy and understand the high-tech world. Sometimes companies come to the agents thinking that they need an employee with one type of skill when, in reality, the employee should have other technical skills. Agents must assess the company's needs and the crucial aspects of projects. Sometimes agents may have to do research to determine what the most important requirements are for certain projects. Then agents can make recommendations about what type of talent the company needs and suggest an appropriate match.

Since digital agents work with quite a number of different talents and companies, they get a wide variety of experiences. Working in the high-tech world also offers the opportunity to work with highly creative people, which Hughes finds one of the best aspects of the job. However, working with so many different people, various needs, and technical information can be stressful. "This job can involve a lot of pressure," Hughes says. "My talent relies on me for their livelihood. I'm under pressure to get them their next contract."

REQUIREMENTS
High School
Most people entering technology-related fields have at least a bachelor's degree. If you are considering a career as a digital agent, you should take a college preparatory course load in high school. Naturally, take as many computer classes as you can. This way you'll be able to learn about using computers as well as test out how well you

like working with them. Take mathematics and business courses to prepare you for college and working life. It will be very important to take English or communication courses since much of your work will involve speaking with and listening to people as well as doing research. Consider taking psychology classes, which can help you understand working with people.

Postsecondary Training
Digital agents may have bachelor's degrees in computer-related areas, or they may have liberal arts degrees and extensive computer knowledge. Whatever degree you decide to get, make sure your education includes courses beyond computer and Web work. Take business classes, because you will be working with budgets and finances. Human resource courses will teach you about working with people. Psychology and English courses will also be beneficial.

Internships or summer jobs with high-tech companies can give you invaluable experience. When you are in the process of choosing a college or university to attend, find out if the placement center will be able to help you locate an internship or summer job with a high-tech company or a large company that needs help in its technical division. Hands-on experience will add to your knowledge as well as give you credibility as an agent looking to place people in this field.

Certification or Licensing
While there is no certification for the position of digital agent itself, there are numerous certifications available in programming and Web-related skills. You may need to take training courses, and to become certified in that skill, you must typically pass a written test. This is a good way to update your skills and remain familiar with new developments in the industry. The more computer knowledge you have, the better equipped you will be to serve your clients.

In addition, some agencies require their agents to be certified in human resources. The HR Certification Institute offers three designations: the professional in human resources, the senior professional in human resources, and the global professional in human resources. See the end of this article for contact information for the HR Certification Institute.

Other Requirements
Like almost every career in the computer field, digital agents must be lifelong learners. To be successful, you must have the desire and initiative to keep up-to-date on new technology and the changes in

the business world and the Web industry. You will also need good verbal and written communication skills. In addition, you must be a good listener and have the ability to relate to many different groups of people. Tuning in to your client's needs is the key to a successful, long-standing relationship. "You must be a good judge of character," says Bill Hughes. "Plus, you must be an astute business person. You need to be able to form trusting relationships and yet not be afraid of rejection."

EXPLORING

There are several ways you can explore this type of work. Test your interest in computers by joining a computer users group or club at your high school or in the local community. Does your school have a website? If not, talk to the principal about designing one. If it does, get involved with the people who update the site and volunteer to help.

Do some research on the latest in computer technology. Examine websites, books, and Internet chat groups that provide good computer education material. Attend computer trade shows and learn about recent developments. Of course, you should take computer classes at your school, but you should also check out what classes are available through community offerings. The local college, for example, may offer an evening class in website design that your high school does not.

Simply accessing the Internet frequently and studying different website designs and the increasing number of e-commerce sites can give you an insight into today's technology and how rapidly the computer industry is changing. Also, ask your guidance counselor or computer teacher to arrange for a computer consultant, Web designer, or programmer to give a career talk at your school. Ask if you can "shadow," or accompany, a professional for a day.

Try getting a part-time or summer job working in a computer store. In this setting you can meet people involved in many aspects of the computer world, from the programmer, to the seller, to the user. You can also get experience in the field of human resources by working at a temporary staffing agency. You may just be answering phones and filing, but you will see how professionals in the resource field work.

EMPLOYERS

Digital agents may work for themselves, for traditional job placement agencies, or for agencies that specialize in working with the high-tech world. In the past few years, traditional placement agencies have come to realize that there is a market in placing highly skilled computer and Web specialists with companies who need this expertise. They are also discovering that more and more companies need temporary or permanent Internet-related personnel but lack the time, resources, or Web savvy to find good people on their own.

While those working at traditional placement agencies may not be known as "digital agents," they may be able to specialize in working in the high-tech sector. Placement services are found across the country, but major cities with a high concentration of Internet and technology specialists can provide the most opportunities.

STARTING OUT

High-tech placement and digital agent work is still too new for there to be any set career path for those interested. However, a combination of human resource, business, and computer experience seems to be the most logical route to this field. Talent and initiative are key attributes for success. Bill Hughes suggests starting out as a commissioned recruiter in a traditional placement agency or working in the human resources department of a company.

A college internship or summer job with a high-tech company may also give you contacts in the field. Use these contacts as well as your school's career services office when you are looking for work. People you meet through computer user groups or at computer trade shows may also know of job openings. Classified ads, employment agencies, and Internet job listings can also provide some possible employment leads.

ADVANCEMENT

Because the career of digital agent is new, advancement opportunities aren't clearly defined and may also depend on the individual agent's goals. One agent may decide he wants to go into Web design himself. Another may decide she wants to start her own agency. However, the beginning digital agent may advance by simply establishing a reputation for good placements and increasing his or her clientele base. As with almost any career, agents who excel at their jobs can generally expect to move up to executive managerial or supervisory positions.

EARNINGS

No government statistics are available for the earnings of digital agents. Industry experts, however, estimate that successful agents can earn anywhere from $70,000 to more than $100,000 a year.

"Digital agents who have a year of experience may make around $40,000 a year," says Bill Hughes.

Typical benefits may be available for full-time employees, including health, life, and disability insurance; sick leave; and vacation pay. Retirement plans may also be available, and some companies may match employees' contributions. Some companies may also offer stock-option plans.

WORK ENVIRONMENT

Digital agents can generally expect to work in a clean office environment. Many people in employment placement and talent agency firms often work over 40 hours a week. In addition, anyone working so closely with the computer industry must remain up-to-date on computer and Internet technology.

OUTLOOK

According to the U.S. Department of Labor, five of the 20 fastest-growing occupations through 2012 are computer related. Since the work of the digital agent is so specialized, this field will probably continue to be relatively small. However, the number of agents can be expected to increase as the Web industry grows in scope.

FOR MORE INFORMATION

Check out this professional organization's website for industry information.

American Society for Information Science and Technology
1320 Fenwick Lane, Suite 1510
Silver Spring, MD 20910
Tel: 301-495-0900
http://www.asis.org

This organization offers various levels of certification for those interested in human resource work.

HR Certification Institute
Society for Human Resource Management
1800 Duke Street
Alexandria, VA 22314
Tel: 703-548-3440
Email: info@hrci.org
http://www.hrci.org

Graphics Programmers

QUICK FACTS

School Subjects
Art
Computer science

Personal Skills
Artistic
Technical/scientific

Work Environment
Primarily indoors
Primarily one location

Minimum Education Level
Bachelor's degree

Salary Range
$37,170 to $62,980 to
$100,980

Certification or Licensing
Voluntary

Outlook
About as fast as the average

DOT
030

GOE
02.06.01

NOC
2162

O*NET-SOC
15-1021.00

OVERVIEW

Graphics programmers design software that allows computers to generate graphic designs, charts, and illustrations for manufacturing, communications, entertainment, and engineering. They also develop computer applications that graphic designers use to create multimedia presentations, posters, logos, layouts for publication, and many other objects.

HISTORY

Developed from technology used during World War II, the first modern computer was used in 1951 to organize the population data compiled in the 1950 U.S. Census. At that time, computers were considered nothing more than electronic systems for storing and retrieving information. Because of their immense size and development costs, plus the difficulty of installing and programming them, it was thought that computers would only be useful for huge projects such as a nationwide census. But private companies were quick to explore ways to harness the power of the computer to gain an edge over their competitors. Today, computer technology has been adapted for use in practically every field and industry, from manufacturing to medicine, from telephones to space exploration, from engineering to entertainment.

Computers are used not only to store and organize data; they also communicate data to other computers and to users. Computer scientists have made great strides in adapting computer technology for visual presentation. Graphics are an important communications tool and are now used in many diverse industries to interpret and display the relationships between various data elements. They can be used to illustrate difficult or abstract concepts, show ratios and proportions, or demonstrate how forces such as the weather change over time. As the graphics field has expanded, the emphasis has shifted from two-dimensional solutions, such as brochures or posters, to three-dimensional design, including screen displays for television and Web pages. Computer graphics can also be used for interactive automobile design, medical simulations, animation, flight simulations, digital movie special effects, and virtual reality.

Although "hand skills," such as drawing and drafting are still used in graphics design, the computer has become the primary tool. The advantages of using computers are many, including speed, precision, and on-screen editing.

THE JOB

The graphics programmer's job is similar to that of other computer programmers: determining what the computer will be expected to do and writing instructions for the computer that will allow it to carry out these functions. For a computer to perform any operation at all, detailed instructions must be written into its memory in a computer language, such as BASIC, COBOL, PASCAL, C++, HTML, Smalltalk, and Java. The programmer is responsible for telling the computer exactly what to do.

A graphics programmer's job can be illustrated by tracing how a program designed for desktop publishing is developed. Working with a computer systems analyst, the graphics programmer's first step is to interview managers or clients to determine the kinds of tasks the program will be expected to perform, such as drawing shapes, organizing text, and adding different colors. The programmer investigates current computer graphics capabilities and how to improve them.

Once the expectations of the program are identified, the programmer usually prepares a flowchart, which illustrates on paper how the computer will process the incoming information and carry out its operations. The programmer then begins to write the instructions for the computer in a programming language, such as FORTRAN or C. The coded instructions will also contain comments so other programmers can understand it.

Once the program is written, it is tested thoroughly by programmers, graphic designers, and quality assurance testers to make sure it can do the desired tasks. If problems, or glitches, do exist, the program must be altered and retested until it produces correct results. This is known as debugging the program.

Once the program is ready to be put into operation, the programmer prepares the written instructions for the people who will be operating and consulting the graphics program in their daily work.

Many diverse industries use computer graphics. In medicine, for example, physicians, nurses, and technicians can use computer graphics to view patients' internal organs. Scanners feed vital information about a patient's body to a computer that interprets the input and displays a graphic representation of the patient's internal conditions. Computer graphics are used in flight simulators by airlines and NASA to train pilots and astronauts. Weather forecasters and television newscasters use graphics to explain statistical information, such as weather or stock market reports. Business people use computer-generated graphs and charts to make their reports more interesting and informative. Engineers use computer graphics to test the wear and stress of building materials and machine parts. The movie industry has found ingenious ways to use computer graphics for special effects. Professional artists have explored computer graphics for creating works of art.

Graphics programmers can be employed either by software manufacturing companies or by the companies that buy and use the software (known as the end user.) The programmer who works for a software manufacturer will work on programs designed to fit the needs of prospective customers. For example, the programmer might work on a report-writing program for businesses, and so develop simple ways for people to display and print statistical data in the form of diagrams, pie charts, and bar graphs. Programmers, working alone or as part of a team, must make the product user friendly.

Computer graphics programmers who work for end users have to tailor commercial software to fit their company's individual needs. If a company has limited computer needs or cannot afford to keep a programmer on payroll, it can call an independent consulting firm that has graphics programmers on staff and hire consultants for specific projects.

REQUIREMENTS

High School

If you are interested in computer graphics programming, take classes that satisfy the admission requirements of the college or university that you plan to attend. Most major universities have requirements for English, mathematics, science, and foreign languages. Other classes that are useful include physics, statistics, logic, computer science, and if available, drafting. Since graphics programmers have to have an artistic sense of layout and design, art and photography courses can also be helpful.

Postsecondary Training

A bachelor's degree in computer science or a related field is essential for anyone wishing to enter the field of computer graphics programming. It is not a good idea, however, to major in graphics programming exclusively, unless you plan to go on to earn a master's degree or doctorate in the field. According to the Special Interest Group on Computer Graphics, a division of the Association for Computing Machinery (ACM SIGGRAPH), it is better for you to concentrate on the area in which you plan to use computer graphics skills, such as art or engineering, rather than focusing on graphics classes.

Others complete a general computer science curriculum, choosing electives such as graphics or business programming if they are available. Because there are many specialties within the field of computer graphics, such as art, mapmaking, animation, and computer-aided design (CAD), you should examine the courses of study offered in several schools before choosing the one you wish to attend. An associate degree or a certificate from a technical school may enable you to get a job as a keyboard operator or other paraprofessional with some firms, but future advancement is unlikely without additional education. Competition for all types of programming jobs is increasing and will limit the opportunities of those people with less than a bachelor's degree.

Certification or Licensing

No specific certification is available for graphics programmers. One general computer-related certification (certified computing professional) is available from the Institute for Certification of Computing Professionals, whose address is listed at the end of this article. Although it is not required, certification may boost your attractiveness to employers during the job search.

Other Requirements

Successful graphics programmers need a high degree of reasoning ability, patience, and persistence, as well as an aptitude for mathematics. You should also have strong writing and speaking skills, so that you can communicate effectively with your coworkers and supervisors.

EXPLORING

If you are interested in a career in computer graphics programming, you might want to check out *Computer Graphics Quarterly*, a publication of the Special Interest Group on Computer Graphics. You can read back issues of this interesting publication online at http://www.siggraph.org/publications/newsletter.

You might also contact the computer science department of a local university to get more information about the field. It may be possible to speak with a faculty member whose specialty is computer graphics or to sit in on a computer graphics class. Find out if there are any computer manufacturers or software firms in your area. By contacting their public relations departments, you might be able to speak with someone who works with or designs computer graphics systems and learn how one works.

If you are interested in the artistic applications of graphics, get involved with artistic projects at school, like theater set design, poster and banner design for extracurricular activities, or yearbook or literary magazine design.

EMPLOYERS

Graphics programmers are employed throughout the United States. Opportunities are best in large cities and suburbs where business and industry are active. Programmers who develop software systems work for software manufacturers, many of which are in central California. There is also a concentration of software manufacturers in Boston, Chicago, and Atlanta. Programmers who adapt and tailor the software to meet specific needs of clients are employed around the country by the end users.

Graphics programmers can also work in service centers that furnish computer time and software to businesses. Agencies, called job shops, employ programmers on short-term contracts. Self-employed graphics programmers can also work as consultants to small companies that cannot afford to employ full-time programmers.

STARTING OUT

Counselors and professors should be able to keep you informed of companies hiring computer programmers, including graphics programmers. Large manufacturing companies and computer software firms who employ many computer programmers send recruiters to universities with computer science departments, usually working cooperatively with the guidance and career services departments. Guidance departments can also tell you about any firms offering work-study programs and internships, which are excellent ways to gain training and experience in graphics programming. As employers become increasingly selective about new hires and seek to hold down the costs of in-house training, internships in computer programming are a great opportunity not only for on-the-job experience but also for a possible position after graduation from college.

Other possible sources of entry-level jobs are the numerous placement agencies that specialize in the field of computers. These agencies often advertise in major newspapers, technical journals, and computer magazines. They can also help match programmers to temporary jobs as more firms lower their personnel costs and hire freelance programmers to meet their needs. Programmers can also find out about new job opportunities by attending computer graphics conferences and networking with their professional peers. Some job openings are advertised in newspapers or online.

ADVANCEMENT

The computer industry experiences high turnover, as large numbers of programmers and other employees change companies and/or specialties. Some programmers leave their positions to accept higher paying jobs with other firms, while others leave to start their own consulting companies. These extremely mobile conditions offer many opportunities both for job seekers and for those looking for career advancement.

In most companies, especially larger firms, advancement depends on an employee's experience and length of service. Beginning programmers might work alone on simple assignments after some initial instruction or on a team with more experienced programmers. Either way, beginning programmers generally must work under close supervision.

Because technology changes so rapidly, programmers must continuously update their training by taking courses sponsored by their employers or software vendors. For skilled workers who keep up to date with the latest technology, the prospects for advancement are good. In large organizations, they can be promoted to lead programmer and given supervisory responsibilities. Graphics programmers might be promoted to programmer-analysts, systems analysts, or to managerial positions. As employers increasingly contract out programming jobs, more opportunities should arise for experienced programmers with expertise in specific areas to work as consultants.

EARNINGS

According to the National Association of Colleges and Employers, starting salary offers in computer science averaged $47,419 in 2003. The U.S. Department of Labor reports that median annual earnings of computer programmers were $62,980 in 2004. The lowest paid 10 percent earned less than $37,170; the highest 10 percent earned more than $100,980.

Programmers who work as independent consultants earn high salaries, but their salary may not be regular. Overall, those who work for private industry earn the most. Industry offers graphics programmers the highest earnings, as opportunities have expanded in aerospace, electronics, electrical machinery, and public utilities. Most of the best opportunities in this field are found in the Silicon Valley in northern California or in Seattle, Washington, where Microsoft has its headquarters.

Those who work for corporations or computer firms usually receive full benefits, such as health insurance, paid vacation, and sick leave.

WORK ENVIRONMENT

Most programmers work with state-of-the-art equipment. They usually put in eight to 12 hours a day and work a 40- to 50-hour week. To meet deadlines or finish rush projects, they may work evenings and weekends. Programmers work alone or as part of a team and often consult with the end users of the graphics program, as well as engineers and other specialists.

Programmers sometimes travel to attend seminars, conferences, and trade shows. Graphics programmers who work for software manufacturers may need to travel to assist current clients in their work or to solicit new customers for the software by demonstrating and discussing the product with potential buyers.

Graphics programmers in visual illustration departments of film or television production may spend months designing graphics for a clip that lasts minutes. There is often considerable pressure due to these deadlines.

OUTLOOK

According to the U.S. Department of Labor, the demand for computer specialists should be strong for the next decade, but the employment for programmers is slower than other areas of computer science. Technological developments have made it easier to write basic code, eliminating some of the need for programmers to do this work.

More sophisticated software has allowed more and more end users to design, write, and implement more of their own programs. As a result, many of the programming functions are transferred to other types of workers. In addition, programmers will continue to face increasing competition from international programming businesses where work can be contracted out at a lower cost.

However, the specialty of graphics programming should still have a promising future. As more applications for computer graphics are explored and businesses find ways to use graphics in their everyday operations, graphics programmers will be in demand.

FOR MORE INFORMATION

For timelines, photos, and the history of computer developments, visit or contact
  Computer History Museum
  1401 North Shoreline Boulevard
  Mountain View, CA 94043
  Tel: 650-810-1010
  http://www.computerhistory.org

For information on certification, contact
  Institute for Certification of Computing Professionals
  2350 East Devon Avenue, Suite 115
  Des Plaines, IL 60018-4610
  Tel: 800-843-8227
  Email: office@iccp.org
  http://www.iccp.org

For information on careers and education, student memberships, and the student newsletter looking.forward, *contact*
  IEEE Computer Society
  1730 Massachusetts Avenue, NW
  Washington, DC 20036-1992
  Tel: 202-371-0101
  http://www.computer.org

For information on membership, conferences, and publications, contact ACM SIGGRAPH.
  Special Interest Group on Computer Graphics (SIGGRAPH)
  Association for Computing Machinery
  1515 Broadway, 17th Floor
  New York, NY, 10036
  http://www.siggraph.org

Help Desk Representatives

QUICK FACTS

School Subjects
Business
Computer science

Personal Skills
Communication/ideas
Helping/teaching
Leadership/management

Work Environment
Primarily indoors
Primarily one location

Minimum Education Level
Some postsecondary training

Salary Range
$32,000 to $40,000 to
$55,632

Certification or Licensing
Voluntary

Outlook
Faster than the average

DOT
033

GOE
02.06.01

NOC
2282

O*NET-SOC
15-1041.00

OVERVIEW

Help desk representatives help computer users by advising them on how to solve problems relating to their computers, software, or peripheral devices. Help desk positions include *call routing specialists, help desk representatives, level one support specialists, level two support specialists,* and *help desk managers.* Computer support in general is challenging work, usually requiring the employee to help frustrated users solve problems in a timely manner. The job requires the representative to use a combination of psychology and analytical problem-solving skills. Help desk representatives need strong communication and technical skills. The U.S. Department of Labor classifies help desk representatives under the general category of computer support specialists. There are approximately 507,000 computer support specialists employed in the United States.

HISTORY

Technical support has been around since the development of the first computers. But it has only been in the last 25 years that help desk representatives and other support specialists have become an integral part of the computer and Information Technology (IT) industries. In an attempt to gain customer loyalty, more computer and IT companies are offering free or reasonably priced technical support as part of the purchase package. Additionally, the number of home computer users with support issues has skyrocketed over the past decade. Technological innovations and the variety of hardware, software, and online services available to businesses and consumers have also created strong demand for help desk representatives.

THE JOB

It is the responsibility of a help desk representative to assist users of a company's online services with computer- and service-related issues. These specialists are faced with the task of simplifying technical issues for users of the company's services and, ultimately, for ensuring the satisfaction of every user who is having enough trouble to call for help. In very large businesses, there might be enough need for online services help to warrant the creation of an internal support group for that purpose. *Internal help desk representatives* help users from their own company with online services. *External help desk representatives* offer aid to the company's customers.

Whether representatives are internal or external, they usually provide assistance over the phone. A customer or user experiencing a problem will call the representative for help. The person who initially takes the phone call, usually called a *call routing specialist,* will try to determine the general nature and importance of the customer's problem by asking a number of questions. The person in this job must determine the severity and type of the customer's problem and decide upon the best department or individual to handle the call. In most departments, the telephone systems allow for the placement of the call into a queue so that callers will wait on hold until a representative is available to handle their call.

The job of the help desk representative is to pinpoint the exact nature of the customer's problem and then go about helping the customer to fix the problem, or at least determine a course of action to follow the phone call. This work can be very difficult for a number of reasons. The customer may be upset and unable to describe clearly what the problem is, which can hinder the problem-solving process. The help desk representative will need patience and understanding to deal with the customer's frustration and to communicate effectively with the customer. Kate Cain is practice systems project manager at Chicago's Kirkland & Ellis, a large, international law firm that provides extensive online services both internally and externally. Cain's department provides online help desk support as well as help desk support in other arenas. Cain says a typical day in the life of a help desk representative is "very hectic—phones ringing constantly and technicians scrambling to respond to issues and requests." The job is often stressful and challenging.

Because help desk representatives work with people over the phone, they are unable to see the customer's computer screen. To understand the problem, the representative must ask detailed questions. Some help desks develop scripts to aid the representatives in quickly categorizing and isolating the nature of the problem; other situations may require the representative to use his or her analytical skills and experience to get to the solution.

Some help desk departments have different levels of support based on the expertise required to solve a problem. In these cases, customers may initially speak with a *level one support specialist* or *representative*, who has general, less specialized technical experience. If these specialists are able to isolate the problem to a particular area but unable to solve it, they may refer the customer to a *level two support specialist* or *representative* who works with that particular area. These representatives have greater knowledge and experience with a few areas of expertise and are more qualified to handle complicated issues.

Help desk managers typically oversee the work of help desk representatives as well as working on technical issues themselves. Their managerial duties may include training new employees, reviewing representatives' work, and meeting with other company department heads to keep up with new developments and company goals. Almost all help desk departments make recordings of the phone calls they receive asking for help. Managers may use these recordings when training new employees and for monitoring the effectiveness of their current employees.

Response time is another critical factor in evaluating the effectiveness of help desk departments. At more sophisticated departments, computers track the amount of time a customer waits before speaking to a representative, the number of customers who give up waiting before their call is answered, and the amount of time the customer spends with a representative. The statistics may be tracked for each employee to be used in evaluating job performance. Many help desk departments relay the average hold time data to their customers who are waiting on hold to give them an idea of how much time they will have to wait.

In addition to their telephone support services, most help desk departments offer the option of having questions answered by email. Customers may send emails describing their problems to an address something like support@anycompany.com. Emails will arrive at the business and may be sorted by hand or by machine, based on the subject line. There may be help desk representatives dedicated to answering the email questions, or it may simply be the occasional duty of all representatives to help with this task.

In high-tech businesses, customers may also be given the option of receiving online support. This type of support will usually be accomplished through a special website where the customer will engage in

Best Web Support Sites of 2005

Strong online customer service and support is one of the keys to success in the highly competitive computer and online support industry. To recognize excellence in support, the Association of Support Professionals (ASP) oversees an annual competition. It evaluates sites using the following criteria: overall usability, design, and navigation; knowledgebase and search implementation; interactive features; personalization; and major site development challenge. The 2005 winners (in alphabetical order) were

- BEA Systems
- Cisco Systems
- Cognos
- Interwoven
- McKesson ECSG
- Microsoft
- Pervasive Software
- tink3
- Xilinx

You can learn more about the winners by picking up a copy of *The Year's Ten Best Web Support Sites* from the ASP. Visit http://www.asponline.com for details.

a live "chat" session with a help desk representative. Naturally, this option assumes that the customer is still able to connect and use the online services. Online support has the advantage of allowing the representative to handle several customers at once.

At some companies, customers may need the option of receiving support 24 hours a day, seven days a week. At these companies the help desk typically will be run in three eight-hour shifts per day.

REQUIREMENTS

High School

The minimum formal education requirement for help desk representatives is a high school diploma, although you should also expect, at a minimum, some on-the-job training. In high school, courses in computer science, math, and electronics will be useful, but don't underestimate the importance of people skills in this job. An understanding of psychology and strong communication skills are important when your work involves working closely with people who are having problems and often are distraught or angry. You'll also need a mastery of English and speech, so take these classes. As a help desk representative, you'll need not only technical knowledge, but also the ability to explain procedures and give instructions in a way that's easily understood, often to people who have little technical knowledge or experience. Depending on the nature of your job, you might have to provide assistance online (in writing) or orally (over the phone).

Postsecondary Training

Because the computer/online industry is constantly evolving and there are new products and services emerging every day, an interest and ability to keep pace with the changes and learn quickly are generally valued more highly than one's level of education. While employers might look favorably on applicants with previous training and education, they know that the most important training a candidate will receive will be on the job. "Constant training is a requirement in the technology area," says Kate Cain. "Technology is constantly and dramatically changing."

Many people consider working as a call routing specialist or help desk representative entry-level jobs. If you wish to advance in this field to senior or managerial positions, you will need to complete some formal education beyond high school. Consider earning an associate or bachelor's degree in computer science or a related technical specialty or participating in a certification program. While your experience, abilities, and attitude will still be key, an advanced education demonstrates your willingness and ability to learn technical processes and indicates the likelihood that you'll bring a certain level of knowledge and proficiency to the job.

Cain's advice is to get as broad experience as possible in the major technical areas before focusing on a specialty. She asserts that familiarity with the many different facets of technology is essential to make the technology work to its fullest potential.

Certification or Licensing

In the computer industry, there is a general standard certification known as "A+" certification. This is a non-product-specific, industry standard certification for computer service people. Usually this certification is for people who are fixing the hardware, but many people working at help desks have it as well. The administering body for this certification is the Computing Technology Industry Association, also known as CompTIA. The Association also offers the CompTIA Network+ certi-

Successful help desk
representatives have
a special combination
of technical skills and
people skills. *(Corbis)*

fication to network support specialists who have at least nine months
of work experience.

Certification specifically for help desk workers, while not yet the
industry norm, is currently a widely debated topic. Those in favor of
certification for help desk representatives assert that there are some
basics ("soft skills"/customer management, various types of technical
training, and so forth) that could be covered in certification programs
and improve workers' competence and efficiency. Others counter that
there are flaws in the concept that keep it from being very useful. A
common complaint about the certification programs that exist is that
there is no continuing education or re-testing required to maintain certification—a special problem in a field that changes rapidly and dramatically. Many would characterize the certification process as a training
program, feeling that calling it professional certification is a stretch.

Currently, there are several certification programs available specific
to help desk representatives, such as those offered by Help Desk Institute and Service and Support Professionals Association. There is no
universally accepted certification program, however. Still, for those

just starting out in the field, these certification programs offer education and exposure, and, more importantly, may open up employment opportunities for those who complete the program.

Other Requirements

If you're interested in becoming a help desk representative, you should enjoy problem solving, work well under pressure, and be able to communicate clearly and politely. Naturally, a help desk representative will need technical skills, experience, and understanding. The most successful help desk representatives, though, have a special combination of technical skills and people skills.

Remember, you'll often be dealing with people who are frustrated and even angry. Cain says, "People do not call the help desk because they are having a good day. They call because something is wrong or broken. Often, the help desk technician is the recipient of users' pent-up frustration. Successful technicians can keep cool under pressure, respond quickly to stressful situations, and don't let much get under their skin."

It is important that help desk representatives stay focused on solving the problem rather than taking the customer's anger personally. Eric Rabinowitz, the founder of Toronto's IHS Helpdesk Service, spent hours interviewing the best help desk analysts he could find to determine what the most important qualities and characteristics are for a person in this field. He found that one of the most important traits is empathy. Frustrated customers want solutions to their problems, yes, but they also want to feel that the person on the other end of the phone cares about helping them. Being a good listener is essential.

Cain also emphasizes the importance of the "soft skills" that are required in this profession. "You not only need to fix what's broken, you need to be able to explain what you are doing in a way that 'non-techies' can understand," she says.

EXPLORING

It's easy to get computer experience these days, so take advantage of every opportunity. You can subscribe to computer magazines, join your school's computer club, surf the Internet—even playing computer or video games can give you a feel for some of the functions of modern technology. Naturally, you'll want to take as much computer science in school as possible; this will help you figure out if you have a natural inclination for the technical arena. Also, look into signing up for more advanced computer classes at a community center or local technical school.

Another good way to experience the job of the help desk representative is to come to it as a customer. You can learn a lot by pitching computer problems or questions to a help desk representative and listening to how he or she responds to your questions. Also, ask your school guidance counselor or computer teacher to arrange for a help desk representative to speak to interested students at a career day.

Finally, try to get a part-time or summer job at a computer store. This job will give you firsthand experience working with customers and computers. If you have enough computer knowledge, you may even be responsible for dealing with the problems customers have with their computers.

EMPLOYERS

According to the U.S. Department of Labor, there are approximately 507,000 computer support specialists, including help desk representatives, working in the United States. Potential employers for help desk representatives range from Internet service providers, such as America Online, to very specific niche-market online information services providers, such as Lexis-Nexis, to businesses with an online presence, such as banks, that provide Internet services to its customers, to companies that offer assistance with the products, such as software manufacturers.

Many of the jobs in this industry are located on the East and West Coasts in large metropolitan areas such as Boston, New York, Los Angeles, and San Francisco. The Midwest and South represent growing markets as well, with many jobs in Chicago, St. Louis, Houston, and Dallas. The Internet's popularity has allowed many businesses to establish help desk call centers in less expensive metropolitan areas like Nashville and Baltimore. Employment is also available abroad.

STARTING OUT

One of the best ways to look for a help desk position is to start with a company you know and like. Browse the company's website for more information about it, available jobs, and the requirements and application process.

You can also scan the want ads in local newspapers for available positions. You may find that employment agencies are a source for jobs in this field. Employment agencies specializing in temporary work also allow you to try jobs for a short period of time without the commitment required of a full-time employee.

Becoming certified as a help desk representative is an excellent way to gain a competitive edge as you seek your first job, and certification programs will also give you contacts in the field and may assist you with job placement.

Of course, nothing is more effective than communicating directly with computer professionals to find out more about the industry and hear about job openings before they become available to the general public. Attending job fairs and industry conventions are good ways to meet professionals who can give you more information.

Once you have completed an associate or bachelor's degree, make use of your school's career services office. The office should be aware of job openings when they are posted and give you assistance with applying for jobs.

ADVANCEMENT

Advancement opportunities are excellent for help desk representatives. Kate Cain says, "If you assert yourself, you will learn a wide variety of skills very quickly—both technical and people skills. Help desk is a terrific starting point in order to gain exposure to the widest variety of technical issues."

An employee who succeeds in a help desk position demonstrates technical skill, diplomacy, good communication skills, and sound judgment—all qualities that translate well into advanced positions with more responsibility and higher salaries. Depending on an individual's interests, he or she might advance to a more sophisticated technical position or veer off into a role in sales, management, or administration. The average tech support person will spend one-and-a-half to two years in the position, plenty of time to learn the ropes, develop skills, and prove his or her worth. Employees who demonstrate an understanding of the company's products, philosophies, and goals will be the best candidates for advancement. The better help desk representatives know their company, the better the chances that they'll have to be recognized as promotable material.

EARNINGS

Salaries for help desk representatives vary depending on their experience, location, and the size and type of company for which they work. A 2004 technical support salary survey by the Association of Support Professionals reported that customer service representatives earned approximately $32,000. Support technicians earned $40,000 and senior support technicians earned approximately $50,000.

According to Salary.com, base annual salaries for help desk workers ranged from less than $35,636 to $46,108 or more in 2004. Annual base salaries for senior help desk workers ranged from less than $42,144 to $55,632 or more.

Managers in some industries, such as those working in health care, may make more than these figures. Pay tends to be highest in the larger metropolitan areas on the East and West Coasts and in Chicago. In addition, help desk representatives usually receive benefits packages. These packages typically include medical and dental insurance, paid vacation, sick leave, and retirement plans.

WORK ENVIRONMENT

These are indoor jobs, usually in high-rises or other dedicated corporate offices. Many help desk representatives work in small cubicles where privacy is at a minimum. A telephone headset is a must for this environment, as help desk representatives will be on the phone 90 percent of their day.

The environment can be noisy, since these workers are surrounded by other representatives who are also talking to customers. Help desk representatives may not be directly supervised on the job, but managers monitor their work for problems throughout the day.

The work schedule for this job is typically a 40-hour week. Overtime is usually handled on a volunteer basis, with extra pay or compensatory time off being the norm for compensation.

Stress management and reduction are important concepts for this industry, as help desk representatives are almost always talking to customers who are not happy and may be agitated. Creative break time activities and seminars will be found at more progressive companies.

Help desk representatives are evaluated by how many customers they handle in a day and how effectively they help in solving customers' problems. Most help desk departments produce reports so the representatives can monitor their own progress in this area.

OUTLOOK

The computer system design and related services industry is one of the fastest growing in the world. Customer support and user satisfaction are vital to the success of these companies; help desk representatives are the linchpins of a successful company offering online services or computer products. The outlook for these jobs is extremely promising, especially during times of economic growth. Even in an economic downturn, however, businesses will still need and demand assistance with these computer issues. The U.S. Department of Labor projects faster than average growth in this category.

These jobs tend to have a fairly short turnaround time. Entry-level employees who excel can quickly climb to the more specialized positions of level two support specialists or to management. Those who are less inclined toward this type of work will quickly find other avenues. The average help desk representative will move on after about two years, leaving gaps to be filled by other promising candidates.

Technology changes rapidly, so a flexibility of knowledge and a willingness to learn new things will be crucial attributes of a successful candidate.

FOR MORE INFORMATION

For salary surveys and other information, contact
Association of Support Professionals
122 Barnard Avenue
Watertown, MA 02472-3414
Tel: 617-924-3944
http://www.asponline.com

For information on certification, contact
Computing Technology Industry Association
1815 South Meyers Road, Suite 300
Oakbrook Terrace, IL 60181-5228
Tel: 630-678-8300
http://www.comptia.org

For information on certification, advice on getting a job, and earnings, contact
Help Desk Institute
102 South Tejon, Suite 1200
Colorado Springs, CO 80903
Tel: 800-248-5667
Email: support@thinkhdi.com
http://www.thinkhdi.com

For information on certification, check out the following website:
Service and Support Professionals Association
11031 Via Frontera, Suite A
San Diego, CA 92127
Tel: 858-674-5491
Email: info@thesspa.com
http://www.thesspa.com

For job hunting resources for technical careers, visit the following website:
Techies.com
http://www.techies.com

Information Brokers

OVERVIEW

Information brokers, sometimes called *online researchers* or *independent information professionals,* compile information from online databases and services. They work for clients in a number of different professions, researching marketing surveys, newspaper articles, business and government statistics, abstracts, and other sources of information. They prepare reports and presentations based on their research. Information brokers have home-based operations, or they work full-time for libraries, law offices, government agencies, and corporations.

HISTORY

Strange as it may seem, some of the earliest examples of information brokers are the keepers of a library established by Ptolemy I in Alexandria, Egypt, in the 3rd century B.C. These librarians helped to build the first great library by copying and revising classical Greek texts. The monks of Europe also performed some of the modern-day researcher's tasks by building libraries and printing books. Despite their great efforts, libraries weren't used extensively until the 18th century, when literacy increased among the general population. In 1803, the first public library in the United States opened in Connecticut.

In the late 1800s and early 1900s, many different kinds of library associations evolved, reflecting the number of special libraries already established (such as medical and law libraries). With all the developments of the 20th century, these library associations helped to promote special systems and tools for locating information. These systems eventually developed into the online databases and Internet search engines used today.

THE JOB

An interest in the Internet and computer skills are important to success as an independent information broker, but this specialist needs to understand much more than just search engines. Information brokers need to master Dialog, Lexis/Nexis, and other information databases. They also have to compile information by using fax machines, photocopiers, and telephones, as well as by conducting personal interviews. If you think this sounds like the work of a private eye, you are not far off; as a matter of fact, some information brokers have worked as private investigators.

A majority of research projects, however, are marketing-based. Suppose a company wants to embark on a new, risky venture—maybe a fruit distribution company wants to make figs as popular as apples and oranges. First, the company's leaders might want to know some basic information about fig consumption. How many people have even eaten a fig? What articles about figs have been published in national magazines? What are the recent annual sales of figs, Fig Newtons, and other fig-based treats? What popular recipes include figs? The company hires consultants, marketing experts, and researchers to gather all this information.

Each researcher has his or her own approach to accomplishing tasks, but every researcher must first get to know the subject. A researcher who specializes in retail and distribution might already be familiar with the trade associations, publications, and other sources of industry information. Another researcher might have to learn as much as possible, as quickly as possible, about the lingo and organizations involved with the fruit distribution industry. This includes using the Internet's basic search engines to get a sense of what kind of information is available. The researcher then uses a database service, such as the Dialog system, which makes available billions of pages of text and images, including complete newspaper and magazine articles, wire service stories, and company profiles. Because database services often charge the user for the time spent searching or documents viewed, online researchers must know all the various tips and commands for efficient searching. Once the search is complete, and they've downloaded the information needed, online researchers must prepare the information for the company. They may be expected to make a presentation to the company or write a complete report that includes pie graphs, charts, and other illustrations to accompany the text.

The legal profession hires information brokers to search cases, statutes, and other sources of law; update law library collections;

and locate data to support cases, such as finding expert witnesses, or researching the history of the development of a defective product that caused personal injury. The health care industry needs information brokers to gather information on drugs, treatments, devices, illnesses, or clinical trials. An information broker who specializes in public records researches personal records (such as birth, death, marriage, adoption, and criminal records), corporations, and property ownership. Other industries that rely on information brokers include banking and finance, government and public policy, and science and technology.

"This isn't the kind of profession you can do right out of high school or college," says Mary Ellen Bates, an independent information professional based in Washington, D.C. "It requires expertise in searching the professional online services. You can't learn them on your own time; you have to have real-world experience as an online researcher. Many of the most successful information brokers are former librarians." Her success in the business has led her to serve as past president of the Association of Independent Information Professionals, to write and publish articles about the business, and to serve as a consultant to libraries and other organizations. Some of her projects have included research on the market for independent living facilities for senior citizens and the impact of large grocery chains on independent grocery stores. She's also been asked to find out what rental car companies do with cars after they're past their prime. "Keep in mind that you need a lot more than Internet research skills," Bates says. "You need the ability to run your business from the top to bottom. That means accounting, marketing, collections, strategic planning, and personnel management."

The expense of the commercial database services has affected the career of another online researcher, Sue Carver of Richland, Washington. Changes in Dialog's usage rates have forced her to seek out other ways to use her library skills. In addition to such services as market research and document delivery, Carver's Web page promotes a book-finding service, helping people to locate collectible and out-of-print books. "I have found this a fun, if not highly lucrative, activity which puts me in contact with a wide variety of people," she says. "This is a case where the Internet opens the door to other possibilities. Much of this business is repackaging information in a form people want to buy. This is limited only by your imagination." But she also emphasizes that the job of online researcher requires highly specialized skills in information retrieval. "Non-librarians often do not appreciate the vast array of reference material that existed before the Internet," she says, "nor how much librarians have contributed to the information age." Carver holds a master's degree in library science and has worked as a reference librarian, which involved her with searches on patents, molecular biology, and other technical subjects. She has also worked as an indexer on a nuclear engineering project and helped plan a search and retrieval system on a separate nuclear project.

REQUIREMENTS

High School
Take computer classes that teach word and data processing programs, presentation programs, and how to use Internet search engines. Any class offered by your high school or public library on information retrieval will familiarize you with database searches and such services as Dialog, Lexis/Nexis, and Dow Jones. English and composition courses will teach you to organize information and write clearly. Speech and theater classes will help you develop the skills to give presentations in front of clients. Journalism classes and working on your high school newspaper will involve you directly in information retrieval and writing.

Postsecondary Training
It is recommended that you start with a good liberal arts program in a college or university, and then pursue a master's degree in either a subject specialty or in library and information science. Developing expertise in a particular subject will prepare you for a specialty in information brokering.

Many online researchers have master's degrees in library science. The American Library Association accredits library and information science programs and offers a number of scholarships. Courses in library programs deal with techniques of data collection and analysis, use of graphical presentation of sound and text, and networking and telecommunications. Internships are also available in some library science programs.

Continuing education courses are important for online researchers with advanced degrees. Because of the rapidly changing technology, researchers need to attend seminars and take courses through such organizations as the Special Libraries Association. Many online researchers take additional courses in their subject matter specialization. Mary Ellen Bates attends meetings of The Society of Competitive Intelligence Professionals (http://www.scip.org), since a lot of her work is in the field of competitive intelligence.

Other Requirements

In addition to all the varied computer skills necessary to succeed as an information broker, you must have good communication skills. "You're marketing all the time," Bates says. "If you're not comfortable marketing yourself and speaking publicly, you'll never make it in this business." To keep your business running, you need persistence to pursue new clients and sources of information. You are your own boss, so you have to be self-motivated to meet deadlines. Good record-keeping skills will help you manage the financial details of the business and help you keep track of contacts.

Sue Carver advises that you keep up on current events and pay close attention to detail. You should welcome the challenge of locating hard-to-find facts and articles. "I have a logical mind," Carver says, "and love puzzles and mysteries."

EXPLORING

If you've ever had to write an extensive research paper, then you've probably already had experience with online research. In college, many of your term papers will require that you become familiar with Lexis/Nexis and other library systems. The reference librarians of your school and public libraries should be happy to introduce you to the various library tools available. On the Internet, experiment with the search engines; each service has slightly different features and capabilities.

Visit Mary Ellen Bates' website at http://www.batesinfo.com for extensive information about the business and to read articles she's written. She's also the co-author of a number of books, including *Building and Running a Successful Research Business: A Guide For the Independent Information Professional* (Medford, N.J.: Information Today, 2003). *Super Searchers Do Business: The Online Secrets of Top Business Researchers* (Medford, N.J.: Information Today, 1999), and *Researching Online For Dummies*. 2d ed. (Hoboken, N.J.: Wiley, 2000).

EMPLOYERS

A large number of information professionals are employed by colleges, universities, and corporations, and gain experience in full-time staff positions before starting their own businesses. Those who work for themselves contract with a number of different kinds of businesses and organizations. People seeking marketing information make the most use of the services of information professionals. Attorneys, consulting firms, public relations firms, government agencies, and private investigators also hire researchers. With the Internet, a researcher can work anywhere in the country, serving clients all around the world. However, living in a large city will allow an online researcher better access to more expansive public records when performing manual research.

STARTING OUT

People become researchers through a variety of different routes. They may go into business for themselves after gaining a lot of experience within an industry, such as in aviation or pharmaceuticals. Using their expertise, insider knowledge, and professional connections, they can serve as a consultant on issues affecting the business. Or they may become an independent researcher after working as a special librarian, having developed computer and search skills. The one thing most researchers have in common, however, is extensive experience in finding information and presenting it. Once they have the knowledge necessary to start their own information business, online researchers should take seminars offered by professional associations. Amelia Kassel, president and owner of MarketingBase (http://www.marketingbase.com), a successful information brokering company, offers a mentoring program via email. As mentor, she advises on such subjects as online databases, marketing strategies, and pricing.

Before leaving her full-time job, Mary Ellen Bates spent a year preparing to start her own business. She says, "I didn't want to spend time doing start-up stuff that I could spend marketing or doing paying work." She saved business cards and established contacts. She saved $10,000 and set up a home-based office with a computer, desk, office supplies, fax, and additional phone lines. To help others starting out, Bates has written Getting Your First Five Clients, available through the Association of Independent Information Professionals.

ADVANCEMENT

The first few years of any business are difficult and require long hours of marketing, promotion, and building a clientele. Advancement will depend on the online researcher's ability to make connections and to broaden his or her client base. Some researchers start out specializing in a particular area, such as in telephone research or public record research, before venturing out into different areas.

Once they're capable of handling projects from diverse sources, they can expand their business. They can also take on larger projects as they begin to meet other reliable researchers with whom they can join forces.

EARNINGS

Even if they have a great deal of research experience, self-employed information brokers' first few years in the business may be lean ones, and they should expect to make as little as $20,000. As with any small business, it takes a few years to develop contacts and establish a reputation for quality work. Independent information brokers usually charge between $45 and $100 an hour, depending on the project. Eventually, an online researcher should be able to make a salary equivalent to that of a full-time special librarian—a 2004 salary survey by the Special Libraries Association puts the national median at $58,258. Some very experienced independent researchers with a number of years of self-employment may make well over $100,000.

Helen Burwell, president of Burwell Enterprises, estimates that the average information broker charges $75 an hour. This hourly rate is affected by factors such as geographic location and the broker's knowledge of the subject matter. Information brokers can make more money in cities like New York and Washington, D.C., where their services are in higher demand. Also, someone doing high-level patent research, which requires a great deal of expertise, can charge more than someone retrieving public records.

Information brokers who work full time for companies earn salaries comparable to other information technology (IT) professionals. Salaries for IT professionals can range from $36,000 for entry-level personnel to more than $90,000 for those with more than 10 years' experience. A full-time information broker who works for a large corporation primarily in the area of competitive intelligence can earn $100,000 annually.

WORK ENVIRONMENT

Most independent researchers work out of their own homes. This means they have a lot of control over their environment, but it also means they're always close to their workstations. As a result, online researchers may find themselves working longer hours than if they had an outside office and a set weekly schedule. "This is easily a 50-

to 60-hour a week job," Mary Ellen Bates says. Online researchers are their own bosses, but they may work as a member of a team with other researchers and consultants on some projects. They will also need to discuss the project with their clients both before and after they've begun their research.

Information brokers employed by companies work in an office environment. Although most of their work takes place at a computer, they may have to make trips to libraries, government offices, and other places that hold information that's not available online. Whether or not they are self-employed, all information brokers spend some time in meetings, where they making presentations of their findings.

OUTLOOK

The Internet is making it easier for people and businesses to conduct their own online research; this is expected to help business for online researchers rather than hurt. Alex Kramer, past president of the Association of Independent Information Professionals, predicts that the more people recognize the vast amount of information available to them, the more they'll seek out the assistance of online researchers to efficiently compile that information. There will be continuing demand for information brokers in marketing, competitive intelligence, legal research, and science and technology.

Employment experts predict that with the growing reliance on computer technology, businesses will be willing to pay top dollar for employees and consultants who are flexible, mobile, and able to navigate the technology with ease.

FOR MORE INFORMATION

For information about library science programs and scholarships, contact
American Library Association
50 East Huron
Chicago, IL 60611
Tel: 800-545-2433
http://www.ala.org

For information on information science careers, contact
American Society for Information Science and Technology
1320 Fenwick Lane, Suite 510
Silver Spring, MD 20910

Tel: 301-495-0900
Email: asis@asis.org
http://www.asis.org

To learn more about the career of information broker, contact
Association of Independent Information Professionals
8550 United Plaza Boulevard, Suite 1001
Baton Rouge, LA 70809
Tel: 225-408-4400
Email: info@aiip.org
http://www.aiip.org

For information on continuing education, contact
Special Libraries Association
331 South Patrick Street
Alexandria, VA 22314-3501
Tel: 703-647-4900
Email: sla@sla.org
http://www.sla.org

Internet Consultants

QUICK FACTS

School Subjects
Business
Computer science

Personal Skills
Communication/ideas
Technical/scientific

Work Environment
Primarily indoors
Primarily multiple locations

Minimum Education Level
Bachelor's degree

Salary Range
$35,000 to $65,000 to
$100,000

Certification or Licensing
Voluntary

Outlook
Faster than the average

DOT
N/A

GOE
N/A

NOC
N/A

O*NET-SOC
N/A

OVERVIEW

Internet consultants use their technological and computer skills to help people or businesses access and utilize the Internet. Their work may include implementing or refining a networking system, creating a website, establishing an online ordering or product support system, or training employees to maintain and update their newly established website. Some consultants work independently, and others may be employed by a consulting agency.

HISTORY

The Internet as we know it has only been around a little longer than a decade. In this short amount of time, the Internet has brought new ways of communicating and selling products and services to customers, without the presence of an actual store or office. With the fast growth of Internet sales and services, companies with a Web presence need people who can help create and manage sites to fit the company's business goals. This created the need for the Internet consultant. Because of constantly evolving technology, the future will require even more specialized and complex skills of Internet consultants.

THE JOB

The job of an Internet consultant can vary from day to day and project to project. The duties can also vary depending on the consultant's areas of expertise. For example, an Internet consultant specializing in creative work may design a website and help a company create a consistent visual message, while a consultant who is a "techie" may get involved with setting up the company's Intranet or Internet connections. The entrepreneurial Internet consultant may help a business establish an online storefront and an online ordering and processing system. Some Internet consultants who have considerable business experience may work with CEOs or other company heads to analyze the company's current use of the Internet and determine what markets the company is reaching.

Some consultants work independently (running their own businesses) and are paid for their work by the hour; others may be paid by the project. Those who work for consulting firms may be salaried employees of the firm. Some businesses may require that the consultants be on-site; this means that they work on a particular project at the company's office for several days, weeks, or months. Many consultants work out of their home offices and only visit the company occasionally.

Frank Smith, an Internet consultant in San Diego, California, started working in this career, because, as he puts it, "I was essentially a computer geek and a technology freak. I was interested in computer technology early on and just continued to learn." Smith has a degree in business administration and was previously employed as a project manager for a manufacturing firm. The appeal of working at different locations, meeting a variety of technological challenges, and working independently, however, enticed him into the field of consulting, as it does many people. Smith added to his computer knowledge by learning many software programs and programming languages. He also took classes that focused on special elements of website design, networking, and image manipulation. Internet consultants must constantly update their knowledge to keep abreast of new technological developments.

Smith says it's not difficult to love his job because there are no typical days and no typical projects. "I may work with a company to develop their Web presence, or I may simply analyze what they are currently doing and give them some tips to make their Internet and networking connections more efficient." One of the first things a consultant may do on a new project for a company is to meet with key people at the company. During the meeting the consultant gathers information on the business and finds out what the company hopes to do through the Internet. "I don't simply design a website and get them on the Internet," emphasizes Smith. "I get a feel for their company and their business. I look at their current marketing, advertising, and sales material and make sure their website will be consistent with their printed material."

This means the consultant's work involves researching, analyzing information, and preparing reports based on their findings. As Smith notes, "This takes time and research. Sometimes I go home from a meeting with a stack of material about the company, and I study it to make sure I am familiar with the company and its focus." Internet consultants must know their clients to be successful. Smith adds, "I believe this is an important business aspect that is sometimes overlooked by consultants and company executives when they go on the Internet."

Internet consultants may also develop the entire Internet setup, including the hardware and software, for their client. The client may be a company that is upgrading their equipment or a company that has never been connected to the Internet before. Some consultants also train company employees to monitor, maintain, and enhance their website.

According to Smith, consultants who have business experience and business degrees, as well as some technical training, will be the most highly sought. "A good consultant needs to have a working knowledge of the business world as well as computer and technological expertise." The consultant with an understanding of business is able to offer clients more thorough service than the consultant who is only a computer whiz. "Many consultants can put together a website for their clients," Smith explains, "however, more and more companies are beginning to look for the consultant who can offer added value, such as business analysis or marketing skills that will enhance their business and its products and services."

Although Smith feels there is currently an abundance of work for Internet consultants, he believes that demand may slow as companies get connected to the Internet and establish their presence. New technologies, however, are constantly being developed. The consultant who keeps up with technical changes will be able to offer new and old clients improved and different services.

Some people may use their computer skills to work as consultants in a sideline business or as a supplement to their part-time or full-time job. Linda McNamara is employed on a part-time basis as a website designer with a government agency in Illinois. In addition to that job, though, she also works as an independent Internet consultant. McNamara partners with another consultant to operate a business that designs and maintains websites for small enterprises in the area.

Although McNamara does not consult on the large scale that Smith does, she, too, emphasizes that consultants need to have good communication skills. "Everyone has a different idea of how they want their website to look," she says. "This requires that I have the ability to listen, communicate, and perform according to expectations."

A group of Internet consultants discuss the implementation of an online ordering system for a major retailer. *(Corbis)*

REQUIREMENTS

High School

If you are considering a career as an Internet consultant, you should take a general high school curriculum that is college preparatory. Make sure you take computer science and business courses. You should also take courses that develop your analytical and problem-solving skills such as mathematics (including algebra and geometry) and sciences (including chemistry and physics). Take English courses to develop the research and communication skills you'll need for this profession.

Postsecondary Training

While a college degree may not be necessary to gain entry into this field, you will find it easier to get the best jobs and advance if you have one. As the high-tech market tightens and becomes more sophisticated, consultants with degrees generally have more opportunities than those with a high school diploma. Some people enter the field with computer-related degrees; others have a liberal arts or business background that includes computer studies. No matter what your major, though, you should take plenty of computer classes, study programming, and play on the Web.

Because consultants are usually responsible for marketing themselves, you should have good business skills and knowledge of market-

Internet Consulting Specialties

Specialty	Percent of All Consultants Working in Specialty
Software design/development	21
Project management	18
Network administration	12
Information systems design	12
Database development	6
Enterprise Resource Planning implementation	5
Data warehouse/data mining	4
Quality assurance	3
E-commerce	2
Hardware development	2
Customer Relationship Management implementation	1
Other	14

Source: *Computerworld*, 2005 Salary Survey

ing and sales, as well as computer knowledge. Therefore, take business and management classes, as well as economics and marketing. The consultant with a broad educational background may have the inside edge in certain situations. More and more clients are looking for consultants who can offer "value-added" services such as business analysis and marketing assistance along with computer skills. As one consultant says, "Just attending college teaches rigorous, valuable lessons that can benefit you and your clients in the real world."

Certification or Licensing
There are numerous certifications and designations available in programming languages, software, and network administration. Some employers may require that consultants have certain certifications. To become certified you will probably have to complete a training course and pass a written exam. Often the company that puts out a new technology, such as new software, will sponsor a training program.

The Institute for Certification of Computing Professionals offers the certified computing professional designation, as well as other designations for different professionals in information technology. To become certified, you must pass various written exams and fulfill certain work experience requirements.

Other Requirements

Internet consultants must be lifelong learners. You should have the desire and initiative to keep up on new technology, software, and hardware. You must also have good communication skills, including good listening skills. Creativity and a good eye for graphic design are also desirable. Because Internet consultants deal with many different people in various lines of work, they must be flexible and have good interpersonal skills. To be a successful consultant, you should be self-motivated and have the ability to work alone as well as with groups. You also need to have the patience and perseverance to see projects through to completion.

EXPLORING

You can explore your interest in computers by getting involved with a computer users group or club in your community or school. If a computer trade show comes to your area, be sure to attend. You'll be able to see new advances in technology and talk with others interested in this field. Search the Web for interesting sites, and look at their source code to see how they were developed. Increase your knowledge by experimenting and learning independently. Check out library books about computers and teach yourself some programming or website design skills. Mastering a Web page authoring program is a good introduction to Web design.

Offer to help people you know set up their home computer systems or do upgrades. Gain experience working with people by volunteering to help seniors or others learn how to use computers at a community center. Try to get a summer or part-time job at a computer store. Large retailers, such as Best Buy, also have computer departments where you might find work. The business experience will be beneficial, even if you are not working directly on the Internet.

By simply accessing the Internet frequently and observing different website designs and the increasing number of e-commerce sites, you can gain an insight into how rapidly the information technology industry is changing. Contact computer consultants, website designers, or programmers in your area and set up an informational interview with them. At the interview you can ask them questions about their educational background, what they like about the work, how they market their business, what important skills someone wanting to enter the field should have, and any other things you are interested in knowing about this work.

EMPLOYERS

Many Internet consultants work independently, running their own consulting businesses. Others may be salaried employees of traditional management consulting firms that have Internet consulting divisions or departments. And still others may be salaried employees of Internet consulting companies.

Independent consultants have the added responsibility of marketing their services and always looking for new projects to work on. Consultants at a firm are typically assigned to work on certain projects.

Clients that hire Internet consultants include small businesses, large corporations, health care facilities, and government institutions. Consultants work all across the country (and world), but large cities may offer more job opportunities. Some consultants specialize in working with a certain type of business such as a hospital or a retail enterprise.

STARTING OUT

Most consultants enter the field by working for an established consulting firm. This way they can gain experience and develop a portfolio and a list of references before venturing out on their own as an independent consultant or moving to a different firm in a higher position. The Internet is a good resource to use to find employment. There are many sites that post job openings. Local employment agencies and newspapers and trade magazines also list job opportunities. In addition, your college's career services office should be able to help you.

Networking is a key element to becoming a successful consultant and requires getting in touch with previous business and social associates as well as making new contacts.

ADVANCEMENT

Internet consultants have several avenues for advancement. As they become known as experts in their field, the demand for their services will increase. This demand can support an increase in fees. They can also specialize in a certain aspect of computer consulting, which can increase their client base and fees. Those working for consulting firms may move into management or partner positions. Consultants who want to work independently can advance by starting their own consulting businesses. Eventually they may be able to hire consultants to work under them. Some consultants leave the field to head up the computer departments or perform website administration for corporations or other agencies. Because of the continuous developments within the Information Technology industry, the advancement possibilities for consultants who continually upgrade their knowledge and skills are practically endless.

EARNINGS

Internet consultants' earnings vary widely depending on their geographic location, type of work performed, and their experience and reputation. Beginning consultants may make around $35,000 per year, while many consultants earn around $65,000 annually. Some consultants have salaries that exceed $100,000 a year.

Many independent consultants charge by the hour, with fees ranging from $45 an hour to well above $100 an hour. According to *Computerworld*'s 2005 Salary Survey, Internet consultants earned an average of $61 an hour in 2005. Consultants who work on contract must estimate the hours needed to complete the project and their rate of pay when determining their contract price. Independent consultants must also realize that not all their work time is "billable" time, meaning that general office work, record keeping, billing, maintaining current client contacts, and seeking new business do not generate revenue. This nonbillable time must be factored into contract or hourly rates when determining annual income.

Although independent consultants may be able to generate good contract or hourly fees, they do not receive benefits that may be typical of salaried employees. For example, independent consultants are responsible for their own medical, disability, and life insurance. They do not receive vacation pay, and when they are not working, they are not generating income. Retirement plans must also be self-funded and self-directed.

WORK ENVIRONMENT

Internet consultants can expect to work in a variety of settings. Depending on the project, independent consultants may work out of their homes or private offices. At other times, they may be required to work on-site at the client's facilities, which may, for example, be a hospital, office building, or factory. Consultants employed by a large or small consulting firm may also spend time working at the consulting firm's offices or telecommuting from home.

Internet consultants generally can expect to work in a clean office environment. Consultants may work independently or as part of a team, depending on the project's requirements.

Consulting can be a very intense job that may require long hours to meet a project's deadline. Some settings where employees or consultants are driven by a strict deadline or where a project is not progressing as planned may be stressful. Many people in the computer field often work over 40 hours a week and may need to work nights and weekends. In addition, Internet consultants must spend time keeping current with the latest technology by reading and researching. Intensive computer work can result in eyestrain, hand and wrist injuries, and back pain.

OUTLOOK

According to the U.S. Department of Labor, five out of the 20 fastest growing occupations through 2012 are computer related. There is currently a large demand for Internet consultants; however, as more and more companies become established on the Web, they may hire their own webmasters and systems specialists. In addition, new software programs are making the development of simple Web pages easier to create without expert help.

Frank Smith notes, "If you don't stay on top of the industry, you quickly become unemployable. The market will mature, and companies will not be struggling to get their website up and running like they are now. Consultants will have to be more competent and offer more to their clients." Good consultants who keep current with technology and who are willing to learn and adapt should have plenty of job opportunities.

FOR MORE INFORMATION

This organization's Education Foundation offers a limited number of scholarships and has information on the tech industry. To learn more, contact

Association of Information Technology Professionals
401 North Michigan Avenue, Suite 2400
Chicago, IL 60611-4267
Tel: 800-224-9371
http://www.aitp.org or http://www.edfoundation.org

To learn more about consulting, contact
  Independent Computer Consultants Association
  11131 South Towne Square, Suite F
  St. Louis, MO 63123
  Tel: 800-774-4222
  Email: info@icca.org
  http://www.icca.org

For certification information, contact
  Institute for Certification of Computing Professionals
  2350 East Devon Avenue, Suite 115
  Des Plaines, IL 60018-4610
  Tel: 800-843-8227
  Email: office@iccp.org
  http://www.iccp.org

Internet Developers

QUICK FACTS

School Subjects
Computer science
Mathematics

Personal Skills
Communication/ideas
Technical/scientific

Work Environment
Primarily indoors
Primarily one location

Minimum Education Level
Bachelor's degree

Salary Range
$30,000 to $61,078 to $80,000

Certification or Licensing
Voluntary

Outlook
Faster than the average

DOT
N/A

GOE
N/A

NOC
2175

O*NET-SOC
N/A

OVERVIEW

An *Internet developer*, otherwise known as a *Web developer* or *Web designer,* is responsible for the creation of an Internet site. Most of the time this is a public website, but it can also be a private Internet network. Web developers are employed by a wide range of employers, from small entrepreneurs to large corporate businesses to Internet consulting firms.

HISTORY

With the explosive growth of the World Wide Web, companies have flocked to use Internet technology to communicate worldwide—with employees, customers, clients, buyers, future stockholders, and so on. As a result, these companies need people who can create sites to fit their needs and the needs of their target audience.

In the early years of the Internet, most information presented was text only with no pictures. Today, a few sites still use a text-only format, but the vast majority have evolved to use the latest technologies, using graphics, animation, video, audio, and interactive forms and applications.

For most companies, the first Internet sites were created and maintained by a sole individual who was a jack-of-all-trades. Today, these sites are often designed, implemented, and managed by entire departments composed of numerous individuals who specialize in specific areas of website work. The Web developer is the individual with the technical knowledge of programming to implement the ideas and goals of the organization into a smoothly flowing, informative, interesting website. Because of evolving technology, Web developers will require more specialized skills and technological expertise in the future.

THE JOB

After determining the overall goals, layout, and performance limitations of a client's website with input from marketing, sales, advertising, and other departments, an Internet or Web developer designs the site and writes the code necessary to run and navigate it. To make the site, working knowledge of the latest Internet programming languages such as Perl, Visual Basic, Java, C++, HTML, and XML is a must. The developer must also be up-to-date on the latest in graphic file formats and other Web production tools.

The concept of the site must be translated to a general layout. The layout must be turned into a set of pages, which are designed, written, and edited. Those pages are then converted into the proper code so that they can be placed on the server. There are software packages that exist to help the developer create the sites. However, software packages often use templates to create sites that have the same general look to them—which is not a good thing if the site is to stand out and look original. Also, no one software package does it all. Additional scripts or special features, such as banners with the latest advertising slogan, spinning logos, forms that provide data input from users, and easy online ordering, are often needed to add punch to a site.

Perhaps the trickiest part of the job is effectively integrating the needs of the organization with the needs of the customer. For example, the organization might want the content to be visually cutting-edge and entertaining, however, the targeted customer might not have the modem speed needed to view those highly graphical pages and might prefer to get "just the facts" quickly. The developer must find a happy medium and deliver the information in a practical yet interesting manner.

REQUIREMENTS

High School

In high school, take as many courses as possible in computer science, science, and mathematics. These classes will provide you with a good foundation in computer basics and analytical-thinking skills. You should also take English and speech classes in order to hone your written and verbal communication skills.

Postsecondary Training

There currently is no established educational track for Internet developers. They typically hold bachelor's degrees in computer science or computer programming—although some have degrees in noncomputer areas, such as marketing, graphic design, library and information science, or information systems. Regardless of educational background, you need to have an understanding of computers and computer networks and knowledge of Internet programming languages. Formal college training in these languages may be hard to come by because of the rapid evolution of the Internet. What's hot today might be obsolete tomorrow. Because of this volatility, most of the postsecondary training comes from hands-on experience. This is best achieved through internships or entry-level positions. One year of experience working on a site is invaluable toward landing a job in the field.

Certification or Licensing

Because there is no central governing organization or association for this field, certification is not required. Certifications are available, however, from various vendors of development software applications. These designations are helpful in proving your abilities to an employer. The more certifications you have, the more you have to offer. The Institute for Certification of Computing Professionals and the International Webmasters Association also offer certification.

Other Requirements

A good Internet developer balances technological know-how with creativity. You must be able to make a site stand out from the sea of other sites on the Web. For example, if your company is selling a product on the Web, your site needs to "scream" the unique qualities and benefits of the product.

Working with Internet technologies, you must be able to adapt quickly to change. It is not uncommon to learn a new programming language and get comfortable using it, only to have to learn another new language and scrap the old one. If you're a quick study, then you should have an advantage.

EXPLORING

There are many ways to learn more about this career. You can read national news magazines, newspapers, and trade magazines or surf the Web for information about Internet careers. You can also visit a variety of websites to study what makes them either interesting or not so appealing. Does your high school have a website? If so, get involved in the planning and creation of new content for it. If not, talk to your computer teachers about creating one, or create your own site at home.

EMPLOYERS

Everyone is getting online these days, from the Fortune 500 companies to the smallest of mom-and-pop shops. The smaller companies might have one person in charge of everything Web related: the server, the site, the security, and so on. Larger companies employ a department of many workers, each one taking on specific responsibilities.

An obvious place of employment is Internet consulting firms. Some firms specialize in Web development or website management; other firms offer services relating to all aspects of website design, creation, management, and maintenance.

The Internet is worldwide; thus, Internet jobs are available worldwide. Wherever there is a business connected to the Internet, people with the right skills can find Web-related jobs.

STARTING OUT

If you are looking for a job as an Internet developer, remember that experience is key. College courses are important, but if you graduate and have lots of book knowledge and no experience, you're going to get a slow start. If at all possible, seek out internships while in school.

Use the Internet to find a job. The search engines of popular websites aimed at job seekers (Yahoo! Hot Jobs, http://hotjobs.yahoo.com; Monster, http://www.monster.com; or CareerBuilder.com, http://www.careerbuilder.com) can be useful. While you're online, check out some of the Internet trade magazines for a job bank or classifieds section.

ADVANCEMENT

The next step up the career ladder for Internet developers might be a move to a larger company where the website presence consists of more pages. Some websites have hundreds and even thousands of pages! Another option is to become a *webmaster*. Webmasters generally have the responsibility of overseeing all aspects (technical, management, maintenance, marketing, and organization) of a website. For more information, see the article "Webmasters."

EARNINGS

An entry-level position in Web development at a small company pays around $30,000. According to *Computerworld*'s 2005 Salary Survey, Web developers had average salaries of $57,017 in 2005. They also received an average bonus of $4,061, which increases their total salary to $61,078. Web developers who have considerable expertise can earn salaries of more than $80,000 annually.

Differences in pay tend to follow the differences found in other careers: the Pacific, Middle-Atlantic, and New England regions of the United States pay more than the North Central, South Atlantic, and South Central regions, and men are generally paid more than women (although this may change as the number of women rivals the number of men employed in these jobs).

Benefits include paid vacation, paid holidays, paid sick days, health insurance, dental insurance, life insurance, personal days, and bonuses.

WORK ENVIRONMENT

Web developers work at computers in comfortable offices. Most of their work is done alone; however, developers consult frequently with webmasters and others who work to write or edit the content of a site.

OUTLOOK

The career of Internet developer, like the Internet itself, is growing at a faster than average rate. As more and more companies look to expand their business worldwide, they need technically skilled employees to create the sites to bring their products, services, and corporate images to the Internet. In a survey of information architects by the Argus Center for Information Architecture, respondents predicted that certification and graduate degrees will become increasingly important in this career. Postsecondary training in Internet technology is growing, including graduate degrees in information design, informatics, interactive arts, human-computer interaction, and communication design. Universities that now offer strong programs in computer science, writing, and design will be developing liberal arts programs in information architecture. Jobs will be plentiful in the next decade for anyone with this specialized training.

FOR MORE INFORMATION

For information on scholarships, student membership, and the student newsletter looking.forward, *contact*

IEEE Computer Society
1730 Massachusetts Avenue, NW
Washington, DC 20036-1992

Tel: 202-371-0101
http://www.computer.org

For certification information, contact
Institute for Certification of Computing Professionals
2350 East Devon Avenue, Suite 115
Des Plaines, IL 60018-4610
Tel: 800-843-8227
Email: office@iccp.org
http://www.iccp.org

For information on certification, contact the following organization:
International Webmasters Association
119 East Union Street, Suite F
Pasadena, CA 91103
Tel: 626-449-3709
http://www.iwanet.org

Internet Executives

QUICK FACTS

School Subjects
Business
Computer science

Personal Skills
Communication/ideas
Leadership/management

Work Environment
Primarily indoors
One location with some travel

Minimum Education Level
Bachelor's degree

Salary Range
$55,090 to $94,390 to $134,405

Certification or Licensing
Voluntary

Outlook
Faster than the average

DOT
N/A

GOE
02.07.01

NOC
0611

O*NET-SOC
11-1011.00, 11-1011.02, 11-1021.00, 11-3021.00, 11-3031.01

OVERVIEW

Internet executives plan, organize, direct, and coordinate the operations of businesses that engage in commerce over the Internet. These upper-level positions include presidents, chief operating officers, executive vice presidents, chief financial officers, chief information officers, and regional and district managers. The majority of Internet executives are employed in large companies in urban areas.

HISTORY

Since the early 1990s, online business, often called e-commerce, has been extended to virtually every industry. Advertising, distance education programs, sales, banking, tax filing, Web conferencing, bill payment, and online auctions are just a few of the business outlets in which the Internet has profoundly played a role. Companies that have developed a Web presence in these industries, either in addition to or as a replacement to a brick-and-mortar-business, need management executives to run their online business dealings just as a normal business needs a CEO. This is the job of Internet executives.

THE JOB

All businesses have specific goals and objectives that they strive to meet, such as making a certain profit or increasing the client base by a certain amount. Executives devise strategies and formulate policies to ensure that these objectives are met. In today's business world, many companies that first began as brick-and-mortar businesses now have a presence on the Internet.

Additionally, many new companies, known as dot-coms, are found only on the Internet. At both types of companies, Internet executives are the professionals who devise ways to meet their companies' objectives—making sales, providing services, or developing a customer base, for example—as they relate to the Internet.

Like executives in traditional companies, Internet executives have a wide range of titles and responsibilities. The positions include president, chairman, chief executive officer (who is sometimes the same person as the president or chairman), chief operating officer, chief financial officer, chief information officer, executive vice presidents, and the board of directors. *Presidents, chairmen,* and *chief executive officers (CEOs)* at companies with an Internet presence are leaders of the companies. They plan business objectives and develop policies to coordinate operations between divisions and departments and establish procedures for attaining objectives. They may review activity reports and financial statements to determine progress and revise operations as needed. They also direct and formulate funding for new and existing programs within their organizations. Public relations plays a big part in the lives of Internet executives as they deal with executives and leaders from other countries or organizations, and with customers, employees, and various special interest groups.

Chief operating officers, or *COOs,* at dot-coms and other companies with an Internet presence are typically responsible for the day-to-day operations of the company. They may work to increase their companies' client base, improve sales, and develop operational and personnel policies. Depending on the type of business, other duties a COO may have include heading departments, such as marketing, engineering, or sales. Usually the COO directly reports to the top executive, whether it is the CEO, chairman, or president. COOs typically have years of experience working in their industry and may also have worked at their particular company for years, moving up the corporate ranks while gaining knowledge about their companies' products and markets. Additionally, they have extensive knowledge of Internet capabilities and technologies available that will help their companies reach goals.

Some companies have an *executive vice president* who directs and coordinates the activities of one or more departments, depending on the size of the organization. In very large organizations, the duties of executive vice presidents may be highly specialized; for example, they may oversee the activities of business managers of marketing, sales promotion, purchasing, finance, personnel training, industrial relations, administrative services, data processing, property management, transportation, or legal services. In smaller organizations, an executive vice president might be responsible for a number of these departments. Executive vice presidents also assist the CEO in formulating and administering the organization's policies and developing its long-range goals. Executive vice presidents may serve as members of management committees on special studies.

Dot-coms and other companies with a presence on the Internet may also have a *chief financial officer* or *CFO*. In small firms, the CFO is usually responsible for all financial management tasks, such as budgeting, capital expenditure planning, cash flow, and various financial reviews and reports. In larger companies, the CFO may oversee financial management departments to help other managers develop financial and economic policy and oversee the implementation of these policies.

Chief information officers, or *CIOs,* are responsible for all aspects of their company's information technology. They use their knowledge of technology and business to determine how information technology can best be used to meet company goals. This may include researching, purchasing, and overseeing setup and use of technology systems, such as Intranet, Internet, and computer networks. These managers sometimes take a role in implementing a company's website.

Management information systems directors oversee computer and information systems for an entire company. They often report to the chief information officer. They may be responsible for managing an organization's employee help desk, recommending hardware and software upgrades, and ensuring the security and availability of information technology services.

Chief technology officers evaluate and recommend new technologies that will help their organization reduce costs and increase revenue. They often report to the chief information officer.

In companies that have several different locations, managers may be assigned to oversee specific geographic areas. For example, a large retailer with facilities all across the nation may have a Midwest manager, a Southwest manager, a Southeast manager, a Northeast manager, and a Northwest manager. In the case of Internet companies, whose territory is not limited by geographical boundaries, managerial responsibilities may be assigned by product or client type instead.

All of these executive and management positions may be available at large companies, while the responsibilities of several of these positions may be combined into one role at smaller companies. Internet executives may work in any of these positions for companies that do business exclusively online or traditional businesses that also have an online presence. The common denominator among these executives is that they are all involved to some extent with figuring out how to use the Internet to enhance the capabilities and profitability of their businesses.

Rob Linxweiler, a consultant to a number of Internet companies in the Chicago area, says, "A downside of the industry is that sometimes it's hard to measure success on a daily or even weekly basis. We may accomplish two or three major projects per year, and those are the milestones by which we judge ourselves. It's possible to get mired in the day-to-day and fail to see the larger picture."

Linxweiler is quick to point out that there are many positives to an Internet executive's job, including working with interesting people. He also adds, "The work may not always be fascinating, but the technologies available can be used in some creative ways to overcome obstacles. I like to apply my creativity to problem solving."

Involvement in Internet commerce adds a new dimension for the consideration of executives. While most executives don't get directly involved in the day-to-day operation of the technology that drives their Internet business, an understanding of the technologies at work is crucial to the performance of their jobs. Executives will likely have to work directly with technology experts, so proficiency with the relevant technologies is a necessity. The combination of technological and business expertise Internet executives have makes these individuals among the most sought-after in the executive job market.

REQUIREMENTS

High School

The educational background of Internet executives varies as widely as the nature of their diverse responsibilities. Many have a bachelor's degree in computer science, business administration, or a liberal arts field such as economics or communications. If you are interested in a management career dealing with the Internet, you should plan on going to college after high school. Take a college preparatory curriculum, including classes in science, history, and government. Be sure to take as many computer science classes as possible so that you have a basic understanding of the technology that is available. Because an executive must communicate with a wide range of people, take as many English classes as possible to hone your communication skills. Speech classes are another way to improve these skills. Courses in mathematics and business are also excellent choices to help you prepare for this career. A foreign language may also be helpful in preparing for today's global business market.

Postsecondary Training

Internet executives often have a college degree in a subject that pertains to the department they direct or the organization they administer. For example, chief executive officers may have business administration degrees, chief financial officers often have accounting degrees, chief information officers often have computer science degrees, and directors of research and development often have engineering or science degrees. All Internet executives are expected to have experience with the information technology that applies to their field. While in college, you should keep up with your computer studies in addition to deciding what type of work interests you. Are you drawn to sales and marketing, for example, or does the actual manufacturing of a product interest you? A good way to find out is to get some hands-on experience through an internship or summer job. Your college career services office should be able to help you in locating such a position with a business or organization that appeals to you.

Graduate and professional degrees are common among executives. Many executives in administrative, marketing, financial, and manufacturing activities have a master's degree in business administration. Executives in highly technical manufacturing and research activities often have a master's degree or doctorate in a technical or scientific discipline.

Certification and Licensing

Voluntary computer- and Internet-related certifications are available from professional associations such as the Institute for Certification of Computing Professionals and the Institute of Certified Professional Managers. These designations are helpful in proving your abilities to an employer. The more certifications you have, the more you have to offer.

Other Requirements

There are a number of personal characteristics that make a successful executive, depending upon the specific responsibilities of the position. An executive who manages other employees should have good communication and interpersonal skills. Rob Linxweiler advises, "Work on your communication skills. There is a surprising level of ambiguity in the technological arena, and the ability to say

Meg Whitman,
president and CEO
of online auction site
eBay, speaks at the
International Consumer
Electronics Show.
(Landov)

what you mean and be understood is crucial." He adds, "Hands-on experience with some technologies is also very important. The technologies change rapidly. It's not really relevant which particular system you have experience with, but an understanding of the basic processes and rules by which computer technologies operate is extremely important."

The ability to delegate work and think on your feet is often key in executive business management. A certain degree of organization is important, since executives often manage many different tasks simultaneously. Other traits considered important for top executives are intelligence, decisiveness, intuition, creativity, honesty, loyalty, and a sense of responsibility. Finally, successful executives should be interested in staying abreast of new developments in their industry and technology.

EXPLORING

To explore your interest in the computer and technology aspect of this work, take every opportunity to work with computers. Surf the Web to visit sites of businesses and organizations and find out what services they offer. Improve your computer skills by joining a users group, setting up your own Web page, and taking extra computer classes at a local community center or tech school.

To get experience as an executive, start with your own interests. Whether you're involved in drama, sports, school publications, or a part-time job, there are managerial and executive duties associated with any organized activity. Look for ways in which you can be involved with planning, scheduling, managing other workers or volunteers, fund-raising, or budgeting. Contact a local business executive—the best source would be one whose company also has a website—and ask for an informational interview during which you can talk with him or her about this career. Some schools or community organizations arrange job shadowing, where interested young people can spend part of a day following selected employees to see what their job is like. Joining Junior Achievement (http://www. ja.org) is another excellent way to get involved with local businesses and learn about how they work. Finally, get a part-time or summer job at a local business to get hands-on experience working in an office environment. Although your job may only be that of cashier, you'll be able to see how the business is organized and run. You may also find a manager or executive there who can act as a mentor and give you advice.

EMPLOYERS

General managers and executives hold 2.7 million jobs in the United States, according to the U.S. Department of Labor. These jobs are found in every industry; however, more than 60 percent of these jobs are in the manufacturing, retail, and service industries—industries that are now heavily involved in the Internet.

Virtually every business in the United States offers executive and managerial positions. Obviously, the larger the company is, the more executive and managerial positions it is likely to have. In addition, companies that do business in larger geographical territories are likely to have more executive and managerial positions than those with smaller territories. Businesses with an Internet presence are the norm in today's market. Almost all large retail businesses have some sort of presence on the World Wide Web, and they find their website an essential part of their customer contact program for both sales and marketing. Besides working at large retail businesses, Internet executives may work in such areas as not-for-profit organizations, small start-up companies, and corporate consulting firms.

STARTING OUT

Executive positions are not entry-level jobs. Generally, those interested in becoming Internet executives start with a college degree and gain a significant amount of work experience. After you have decided what industry you are interested in, your college career services office should be able to help you locate your first job. Many companies also send representatives to college campuses to interview graduating students as potential hires. You may also want to attend recruitment and job fairs to find job openings. In addition, a past internship or summer work experience may provide you with contacts that lead to employment. You should research the field you are interested in to find out what might be the best point of entry.

After you have gained some work experience you may want to consider returning to school for a graduate degree. Or you may be able to work your way up through your organization's management levels. Some organizations have executive management trainee programs available to their employees; other companies may pay for an employee's graduate schooling as long as the employee continues to work for the company. Many executives have master's degrees in business administration, although higher degrees in computer science and related technology fields are becoming more common.

Once you have considerable training and management experience, you can move into an executive level position by directly applying to the corporate management. In addition, some executive search and placement firms specialize in jobs for those involved with the Internet. *Digital agents,* specialists who work only with those seeking technology jobs, may also be a good source of employment leads. See the article "Digital Agents" for more information.

Hiring standards for technology executives are still evolving, but it's clear that simply being well acquainted with the technologies is not enough. You will need significant experience in both business management and technology to meet the requirements of most of these positions.

ADVANCEMENT

Most business management and top executive positions are filled by experienced lower-level managers and executives who display valuable managerial traits, such as leadership, self-confidence, creativity, motivation, decisiveness, and flexibility. Rob Linxweiler says, "Good interpersonal skills are a must. Patience, enthusiasm, and the ability to listen to employees are indispensable skills that are often underrated. The ability to make good decisions and act on them is also vital. These are the building blocks of a strong leader, which is the most important thing an executive can be."

Advancement in smaller firms may come more slowly, while promotions may occur more quickly in larger firms. Advancement may be accelerated by participating in different kinds of educational programs available for managers. These are often paid for by the employer. Managers who take company training programs broaden their knowledge of company policy and operations. Training programs sponsored by industry and trade associations and continuing education courses taken at colleges and universities can familiarize managers with the latest developments in management techniques. In recent years, large numbers of middle managers were laid off as companies streamlined operations. An employee's proven commitment to improving his or her knowledge of the business's field and computer information systems is important in establishing a reputation as a top professional.

Business managers may advance to executive or administrative vice president. Vice presidents may advance to peak corporate positions, such as president or chief executive officer. Sometimes executives go on to establish their own firms.

Many CEOs are moving toward the role of chairman and away from day-to-day operations to focus on higher-level, visionary strategy. The ability to understand and implement solutions based on Internet technologies is essential at this level.

Regardless of the industry, the advancement path of executives at Internet companies is limited only by their interest, abilities, and willingness to work hard.

EARNINGS

Salary levels for Internet executives vary substantially, depending upon their level of responsibility, length of service, and the type, size, and location of the organization for which they work. Top-level executives in large firms can earn much more than their counterparts in small firms. Also, salaries in large metropolitan areas tend to be higher than those in smaller cities.

According to *Computerworld*'s 2005 Salary Survey, chief information officers had average salaries of $134,405 in 2004. They also received an average bonus of $30,017, which increases their total salary to $159,096. Chief technology officers earned average salaries of $129,334, and received an average bonus of $25,305, which increases their total salary to $154,639. According to the U.S.

Department of Labor, computer and information systems managers had median annual earnings of $94,390 in 2004. Salaries ranged from less than $55,090 to more than $120,170.

Benefit and compensation packages for Internet executives are usually excellent and may include stock awards and options, cash incentives in addition to bonuses, company-paid insurance premiums, use of company cars, club memberships, expense accounts, and generous retirement benefits.

Top executives at successful Internet companies see few limits to their earnings potential; salaries into the millions of dollars are not uncommon for CEOs and other key executives.

WORK ENVIRONMENT

Internet executives work in comfortable offices near the departments they direct. Top executives at established companies may have spacious, lavish offices with comfortable desks and chairs, PCs, phones, and even personal support staff. They may enjoy such privileges as having executive dining rooms, company cars, club memberships, and liberal expense accounts.

Executives often travel between the company's various offices at the national, regional, or local levels. Top executives may travel to meet with executives in other corporations, both within the United States and abroad. Meetings and conferences sponsored by industries and associations occur regularly and provide invaluable opportunities to meet with peers and keep up with the latest developments. In large corporations, job transfers between the parent company and its local offices or subsidiaries are common, so executives must be prepared to move for their work.

Executives often work long hours under intense pressure to meet corporate goals. A typical workweek might consist of 55 to 60 hours at the office. Some executives, in fact, spend up to 80 hours working each week. These long hours limit time available for family and leisure activities, but the financial rewards can be great.

OUTLOOK

Employment of Internet executives is expected to grow faster than the average over the next several years as Internet businesses continue to grow and new companies are formed. The demand will be high for candidates with strong managerial skills and a solid understanding of computer and Internet technology. Education and experience will also count for a lot. Many job openings will be the result of promotions, company expansions, or executives leaving their positions to start their own businesses.

The employment outlook for executives is closely tied to the over-all economy. In times when the economy is good, businesses expand both in terms of their output and the number of people they employ. This creates a need for more executives. In economic downturns, businesses often lay off employees and cut back on production, which lessens the need for executives.

There were many highly publicized dot-com failures in the early 2000s. Many experts predict that in the next few years, 80 to 90 percent of dot-coms will either close or be acquired by other companies. The statistics, however, are not likely to deter new Web businesses, especially small businesses that are able to find niche markets, anticipate trends, adapt to market and technology changes, and plan for a large enough financial margin to turn a profit. Traditional brick-and-mortar businesses will also have to implement dot-com marketing plans in order to compete and survive. Analysts anticipate that business-to-business e-commerce will become much more important than business-to-consumer transactions.

FOR MORE INFORMATION

For news about management trends, conferences, and seminars, visit the following website:
American Management Association
1601 Broadway
New York, NY 10019
Tel: 212-586-8100
http://www.amanet.org

For certification information, contact
Institute for Certification of Computing Professionals
2350 East Devon Avenue, Suite 115
Des Plaines, IL 60018-4610
Tel: 800-843-8227
Email: office@iccp.org
http://www.iccp.org

For information on certification, contact
Institute of Certified Professional Managers
James Madison University, MSC 5504
Harrisonburg, VA 22807

Tel: 800-568-4120
Email: icpmcm@jmu.edu
http://cob.jmu.edu/icpm

For information on programs that teach students about free enterprise and business and information on local chapters, contact
Junior Achievement
One Education Way
Colorado Springs, CO 80906
Tel: 719-540-8000
Email: newmedia@ja.org
http://www.ja.org

For general information on management careers, contact
National Management Association
2210 Arbor Boulevard
Dayton, OH 45439-1580
Tel: 937-294-0421
Email: nma@nma1.org
http://nma1.org

There are a number of magazines covering the topics of the Internet, computers, and business. Many are available in print form and online. For a sampling of such magazines, check out the following websites:
Computerworld
http://www.computerworld.com

InfoWorld
http://www.infoworld.com

Internet Week
http://internetweek.cmp.com

PC World
http://www.pcworld.com

Wired
http://www.wired.com

Internet Quality Assurance Specialists

QUICK FACTS

School Subjects
Computer science
Mathematics

Personal Skills
Communication/ideas
Technical/scientific

Work Environment
Primarily indoors
Primarily one location

Minimum Education Level
Bachelor's degree

Salary Range
$25,000 to $66,942 to
$100,000+

Certification or Licensing
Voluntary

Outlook
Faster than the average

DOT
N/A

GOE
N/A

NOC
N/A

O*NET-SOC
N/A

OVERVIEW

Internet quality assurance specialists make sure software, applications, and Internet access are not only user friendly but that they deliver what is promised. For example, anyone who has surfed the Web, found a store site, ordered a sweater, and received exactly the right sweater has benefited from the work of a quality assurance specialist. To do their work, specialists plan and carry out a process of testing, correcting, and retesting the software, applications, and websites. They may work on sites for stores, banks, schools, or any number of institutions or organizations. Some companies have their own quality assurance specialists; other companies may hire quality assurance specialists to work on a project-by-project basis. In either case, quality assurance specialists must have excellent computer skills as well as the ability to solve problems.

HISTORY

E-commerce has become part of almost every industry. Advertising, distance education programs, sales, banking, tax filing, Web conferencing, bill payment, and online auctions are just a few of the business outlets in which the Internet has played a significant role. Companies that have developed a Web presence need Internet quality assurance specialists to help plan, organize, and test websites before they are accessed by the end user.

THE JOB

Internet quality assurance specialists improve and ensure the quality of the Internet experience for end users (that is, the people using the Internet and interacting with websites). Quality assurance specialists test software, Web-based applications, or e-commerce applications before they are released for the public to use. Although quality assurance specialists do not have to be software engineers or developers, the more computer experience they have the more qualified they are for the job. To do this work, they need to have programming knowledge and technical computer experience, particularly with software testing.

One of the main responsibilities of the quality assurance specialist is to break or "crash" a company's new website before the company's customers ever see it. By doing this, the specialist finds any potential problems with the site and makes sure those problems are fixed before the site "goes live," or becomes available for the public to use. Ron Wasson, quality assurance manager for Omni Space Technologies in Dallas, Texas, explains, "This is done by developing a broad testing strategy and then putting the software through its paces, documenting every step and result."

Although it may sound like quality assurance specialists are only involved in testing at the end of a project, that is rarely the case. Specialists are often involved during the early stages of planning and are called in to analyze the technical specifications for a site before the site is even built. The specialists meet with the company's development staff to determine what capabilities the company wants for the site. For example, should a visitor to the site be able to order an item or fill out an application? Wasson says, "Many times the quality assurance specialists participate in product planning and the development process to make sure that certain quality elements are built in right from the start." The quality assurance specialists identify where the weak areas or limitations of the site's specifications may be and then develop a testing strategy. At Wasson's company, the quality assurance specialists and the developers see each other on a regular basis. "We begin our day by meeting with the development staff to determine where we are with testing and what is the priority for that day," says Wasson. "We then proceed to set up the required testing."

The specialist must have a thorough understanding of the company and its goals for the new product as well as strong communication skills. "We must make sure that the Web-based modules we are testing meet product management's specifications for user experience and function. They need to do what they were designed to do," Wasson notes. The testing process involves both staff and technological testing tools that automate the process. Careful documentation is required so that the specialist knows what icons were hit or what keystrokes were entered in what order to cause a problem with the site. Part of this job involves analysis, since specialists must examine their findings. Wasson explains, "After the testing is completed, results are gathered and we determine if the results are what was expected."

The specialists then write detailed reports based on their findings and analysis and give these reports to the company's developers. Once the developers have made a change to correct or improve the product, the testing process starts over. Wasson says, "The next day after the changes are made, the testing is done again to see if the problems were fixed or if any new problems have developed." This process can be time consuming. In addition, Wasson notes, "All of this retesting can be particularly stressful, especially as we get closer to a critical deadline. A lot of planning goes into reaching a certain release date and if problems occur it may mean that we are unable to achieve some goals for our customers."

The final testing for a new website comes right before the site goes live. By this point the site has been fully developed and has undergone installation, meaning the site has been placed on the server where it can be accessed by the public. Before the installation is complete, the quality assurance specialist puts the site through a final test to make sure that all the problems identified earlier were fixed and that the installation process itself hasn't created new ones. Time is usually quite short at this point, so the specialist must have pinpointed just a few tests that will show if the site functions correctly. If there is a problem, the specialist must decide quickly if the problem is so severe that the management should be notified and the opening of the site postponed.

Quality assurance specialists work on the cutting edge of new technology. Because of this, they must constantly improve their skills. "As times and technology change," Wasson says, "the role of quality assurance specialists change as well. Performance and function testing change as the architecture of the product changes." Not everything in the workplace is always positive and runs smoothly. Surprises are, unfortunately, a part of the quality assurance specialist's job. "I don't like finding out at eight o'clock at night that we are not headed down the right path with our testing, and we're not where we need to be," Wasson says. "It means there's a long night ahead." Certain qualities will help the specialist in these cases. "This is where you need to be flexible, persistent, detail-oriented, and analytical," Wasson explains. "Hopefully with all these skills and with the help of others on the team, you can solve the problem. If not, you start all over." Most specialists, however, find the challenges of the job and the successful completion of a project highly rewarding.

REQUIREMENTS

High School

Does working as an Internet quality assurance specialist sound like the job for you? If so, you should take high school classes that will give you a well-rounded education. Naturally you should take computer science courses, especially those that allow you to work with computer graphics, on the Web, or with programming. It will be important for you to develop your analytical and problem-solving skills, so take math classes such as algebra and geometry. Business and marketing classes will help prepare you for work in the corporate world. Be sure to take English classes. These classes will help you develop your research, writing, and speaking skills—skills that will be essential in your work as a quality assurance specialist. Science classes, such as physics and chemistry, will round out your education.

Postsecondary Training

Although some people currently working as Internet quality assurance specialists do not have college educations, most companies today prefer to hire candidates with four-year degrees. And as this job market becomes both more established and more competitive, those with college degrees will have the best opportunities for securing work and gaining advanced positions. Therefore, those in the field recommend you get a bachelor's degree. While you may prepare for this work by getting a computer-related degree, you are not limited to this choice. Interestingly, many people also enter this field with a broad-based liberal arts background and have majors in fields such as economics, history, or even languages, along with computer knowledge. Most quality assurance specialists begin as lower-level associates and obtain much of their training on the job. No matter what your educational background, though, you will need strong analytical and communication skills. The specialist is someone who finds out first if there is a problem with an application and must pass this news along to those who are counting on the product to be finished by a certain time. The specialist must be able to give unpleasant news to people at higher management levels quickly, precisely, and professionally.

Certification or Licensing

There are numerous certifications available in programming languages, software, and network administration. The certification process often involves passing a written test and fulfilling certain experience requirements. Organizations, such as the American Society for Quality and the Quality Assurance Institute, also offer certifications in quality assurance and testing. Some employers may require certain certifications. For those whose employers do not require it, however, certification is still recommended. Those with certification show a commitment to the field and may have an advantage when seeking jobs or promotions.

Other Requirements

You should enjoy learning because you will have to spend your career keeping up on new technology, testing tools, software, and hardware. You must also have good analytical skills and strong verbal and writing skills so that you can explain your testing results to others in the company. Because you may deal with many different people throughout a project, you must have good interpersonal skills. As you reach higher positions of responsibility you must be able to plan activities as well as delegate tasks. You should be able to focus on an assignment, be self-motivated, and have the ability to work alone as well as with groups.

Web Stats

- Sixty-six percent of men and 61 percent of women use the Internet.

- On a typical day in 2004, 70 million Americans logged onto the Internet.

- Eighty-one percent of U.S. teenagers between the ages of 12 and 17 use the Internet.

- Eighty-three million Americans have purchased products online.

- Nearly 81 percent of people who surf the Internet use the Microsoft IE 6.0 Internet browser.

- Monday is the most popular day for online traffic. Saturday and Sunday have the least amount of Internet traffic.

Sources: *Time,* Pew Internet & American Life Project, OneStat.com

EXPLORING

There are several ways you can explore this field. One of the first things you should consider doing is joining a computer users group or club in your community or school. If there isn't such a club, go ahead and start one. You'll meet people with similar interests as well as increase your computer knowledge. Check out your school's website and find out who works on updating it. Volunteer to help out with this work. Or, if your school doesn't have a website, talk to your principal about creating one. Check out other organizations in your community that may also have websites, such as your church or synagogue. Again, if they don't have sites, volunteer to help create them. This activity will give you experience working with the Internet and problem solving.

Since the specialist's job requires communication and people skills, consider activities that will allow you to work with others. Volunteer to teach a computer class at a senior citizens' center. Or, look for paid part-time or summer work teaching computer skills. Computer stores, for example, often offer beginner classes to those who have bought their products. In addition, develop your independent learning skills by checking out programming books from the library and teaching yourself new applications.

Ask your parents or school guidance counselor to help you locate computer professionals in your area so that you can set up an informational interview with them. Even if you can't find a quality assurance specialist, talking to anyone in the field may be useful and give you an insider's view of the industry. Naturally, you should surf the Internet frequently. Study different sites and their functions to get an insight into how rapidly the computer industry is changing and where careers may be going.

EMPLOYERS

Quality assurance specialists may work for software developers, government agencies, or firms specializing in quality assurance work. However, most Internet quality assurance specialists today work at large companies with considerable e-commerce investments. Not all of these companies actually sell products over the Internet; some may be large companies with websites that provide customers with services and information. Some smaller companies may combine quality assurance duties with those of other positions such as site development or project management.

Job opportunities are available worldwide; however, major cities with a high concentration of Internet, technology, and software companies may provide the best opportunities.

STARTING OUT

Internet quality assurance specialists can apply for employment directly to Internet and software companies. Generally, people start in lower-level associate positions and work their way up through experience. Classified ads, employment agencies, and Internet job listings can also provide some possible employment leads. Professional organizations may post job openings on their websites. Your college's career services office and alumni connections may also provide job leads. Networking with others in the computer industry or your community is also a good way to make the contacts that may lead to employment.

ADVANCEMENT

Internet quality assurance specialists advance by gaining experience and performing well in their positions. Many move into supervisory or managerial slots that focus more on analysis and planning than actual testing. Other specialists may advance to programming, website development, or project management. As is common in the high-tech fields, advancement may require additional training or an advanced degree. According to Ron Wasson, quality assurance specialists are in a unique position. "They are in the middle of the process," he says, "so they have the opportunity to learn a lot and gain experience that will move them horizontally or vertically in their career."

EARNINGS

Salaries for Internet quality assurance specialists vary widely and are based on such factors as a person's experience, geographic location, and company size. According to *Computerworld*'s 2005 Salary Survey, Internet quality assurance specialists had average salaries of $66,942 in 2005. Some quality assurance specialists just starting out may make around $25,000 a year, while very experienced specialists may make $100,000 or more. In addition, those who work in large metropolitan areas typically have higher earnings than those who work in small towns or rural settings.

Full-time company employees receive typical benefits, including health, life, and disability insurance; sick leave; and vacation pay.

Retirement plans may also be available, and some companies may match employees' contributions. Some companies may also offer stock-option plans.

WORK ENVIRONMENT

Internet quality assurance specialists can generally expect to work in clean, well-lit offices with high-tech equipment. Depending on the project, they may work independently or as part of a team. This type of job can be very intense and require long hours to complete a project. Some situations where quality assurance specialists are driven by a strict deadline or where testing and development are not progressing as planned may be stressful. Many people in the field often work more than 40 hours a week.

Many high-tech companies, especially smaller ones, have a casual office atmosphere that promotes camaraderie and teamwork. Although larger, established companies may tend to be more traditional, their computer and software departments may offer more relaxed work environments.

In addition, Internet quality assurance specialists who are dedicated to keeping up with technology and the Internet community must spend a considerable amount of time reading, researching, and keeping abreast of computer and Internet technology. Even under good working conditions, intensive computer work can result in eyestrain, hand and wrist injuries, and back pain.

OUTLOOK

Internet quality assurance positions will multiply as more and more companies make e-commerce a vital part of their businesses. At this point, many companies are just now beginning to realize that they need to pay more attention to the quality of their Internet sites. Because the field is so young, few people have had a chance to gain substantial Internet quality assurance experience. That means the field should remain open to talented newcomers over the next several years.

Advances in Internet technology will contribute to the high-tech employment growth. Not only can more go wrong as sites increase in complexity, but also the potential problems become much more serious for the corporations as well as customers. As the stakes in e-commerce rise, the peace of mind provided by quality assurance should be in higher demand.

Although reports show a rapid growth in the Internet economy that has led to a shortage of qualified workers, job security with any one firm may be uncertain. Mergers, acquisitions, business failures, downsizing, and the ever-changing technology of this industry mean that there may be some instability regarding long-term employment with any one firm. However, people who are educated about computers and the Internet, keep up with technology, and continue to learn should not have any problem finding employment.

FOR MORE INFORMATION

For more information on the quality assurance field and certification, contact
American Society for Quality
PO Box 3005
Milwaukee, WI 53201-3005
Tel: 800-248-1946
http://www.asq.org

This organization's Education Foundation offers a limited number of scholarships. For information on these opportunities and other facts about the tech industry, check out the following websites:
Association of Information Technology Professionals
401 North Michigan Avenue, Suite 2400
Chicago, IL 60611-4267
Tel: 800-224-9371
http://www.aitp.org or http://www.edfoundation.org

For certification information, contact
Quality Assurance Institute Worldwide
2101 Park Center Drive, Suite 200
Orlando, FL 32835-7614
http://www.qaiworldwide.org

Internet Security Specialists

OVERVIEW

An *Internet security specialist* is someone who is responsible for protecting a company's network, which can be accessed through the Internet, from intrusion by outsiders. These intruders are referred to as hackers (or crackers), and the process of breaking into a system is called hacking (or cracking). Internet security often falls under the jurisdiction of computer systems engineering and network administration within a company. Any company that has an Internet presence might employ an Internet security specialist. This includes all kinds of companies of all sizes anywhere around the world. Other Internet security specialists work for consulting firms that specialize in Internet security. Internet security specialists are sometimes known as *Internet security administrators, Internet security engineers, information security technicians,* and *network security consultants.*

HISTORY

Hacking first began in the telecommunications industry. Cracking a telephone system was called phreaking and involved learning how the telephone system worked and then manipulating it. As PCs began to hook up to networks via telephone lines and modems, phreaking took on new meaning and the information at risk took on greater importance.

QUICK FACTS

School Subjects
Computer science
English
Mathematics

Personal Skills
Communication/ideas
Technical/scientific

Work Environment
Primarily indoors
One location with some travel

Minimum Education Level
Some postsecondary training

Salary Range
$40,000 to $50,000 to $81,035

Certification or Licensing
Voluntary

Outlook
Faster than the average

DOT
033

GOE
02.06.01

NOC
N/A

O*NET-SOC
15-1071.01

November 2, 1988, is sometimes called Black Thursday by pioneers of the Internet community. On that day, a single program, later called a worm, was released onto the early form of the Internet (then called the ARPANET) and quickly rendered thousands of connected computers useless. The creator of the program, Robert Morris Jr., shocked at how quickly it was spreading, sent an anonymous message to Internet users telling how to kill the worm and prevent it from infecting more computers. Morris was convicted of a federal felony and sentenced to three years probation, 400 hours of community service, and $10,050 in fines.

With the release of the Morris Worm, a group of computer experts from the National Computer Security Center, part of the National Security Agency, gathered to discuss the susceptibility to attack of Internet-connected computers. Out of these meetings, the Computer Emergency Response Team Coordination Center, a federally funded organization that monitors and reports activity on the Internet, was started at Carnegie Mellon University. This is considered the beginning of Internet security.

THE JOB

The duties of an Internet security specialist vary depending on where he or she works, how big the company is, and the degree of sensitivity of the information that is being protected. The duties are also affected by whether the specialist is a consultant or works in-house.

Internet security usually falls under the jurisdiction of a systems engineering or systems administration department. A large company that deals with sensitive information probably has one or two Internet security specialists who devote all of their time and energy to Internet security. Many firms, upon connecting to the Internet, give security duties to the person who is in charge of systems administration. A smaller firm might hire an Internet security specialist to come in and set up security systems and software.

A *firewall* is a system set up to act as a barrier of protection between the outside world of the Internet and the company. A specialist can tell the firewall to limit access or permit access to users. The Internet security specialist does this by configuring it to define the kind of access to allow or restrict.

Primarily, Internet security specialists are in charge of monitoring the flow of information through the firewall. Security specialists must be able to write code and configure the software to alert them when certain kinds of activities occur. They can tell the program what activity to allow and what to disallow. They can even program the software to page them or send them an email if some questionable activity occurs. Logs are kept of all access to the network. Security specialists monitor the logs and watch for anything out of the ordinary. If they see something strange, they must make a judgment call as to whether the activity was innocent or malicious. Then they must investigate and do some detective work—perhaps even tracking down the user who initiated the action. In other instances, they might have to create a new program to prevent that action from happening again.

Sometimes the Internet security specialist is in charge of virus protection or encryption and user authentication systems. *Viruses* are programs written with the express purpose of harming a hard drive and can enter a network through email attachments or infected floppy disks or CD-ROMs. Encryption and authentication are used with any network activity that requires transmission of delicate information, such as passwords, user accounts, or even credit card numbers.

Secondary duties can include security administrative work, such as establishing security policies for the company, or security engineering duties, which are more technical in nature. For example, some companies might deal with such sensitive information that the company forbids any of its information to be transmitted over email. Programs can be written to disallow transmission of any company product information or to alert the specialist when this sensitive information is transmitted. The security specialist also might be in charge of educating employees on security policies concerning their network.

Internet security consultants have a different set of duties. Consultants are primarily in charge of designing and implementing solutions to their clients' security problems. They must be able to listen to and detect the needs of the client and then meet their needs. They perform routine assessments to determine if there are insecurities within the clients' network and, if there are, find ways to correct them. A company might employ a consultant as a preventive measure to avoid attacks. Other times, a consultant might be called on after a security breach has been detected to find the problem, fix it, and even track down the perpetrator.

Secondary duties of an Internet security consultant include management and administrative duties. He or she manages various accounts and must be able to track them and maintain paperwork and communications. Senior consultants have consultants who report to them and take on supervisory responsibilities in addition to their primary duties.

Internet security specialists discuss a new user authentication system after a recent attack by hackers. *(Corbis)*

A benefit of using consultants is bringing new perspectives to an old problem. Often, they can use their many experiences with other clients to help find solutions. The consultant does not work solely with one client but has multiple accounts. He or she spends a lot of time traveling and must be reachable at a moment's notice.

REQUIREMENTS

High School

If you are a high school student and think you want to get into the Internet security industry, first and foremost you need to get involved in computer science/programming classes. Don't just book learn, however. Hands-on experience is key and probably is what will get you your first job. Spend time in the school computer lab, learn how computers work, and dabble with the latest technologies. Most of those employed in the field today began at a young age just playing around. What began as a hobby eventually turned into an enjoyable and challenging career.

If you are interested in management or consulting, a well-rounded educational background is important. You should take classes in mathematics, science, and English. You may also want to take business classes to become familiar with the business world.

Postsecondary Training

College courses show employers that you have what it takes to learn. However, most colleges do not have specific programs in Internet security. Most offer computer science, networking, and programming-related degrees, which are highly recommended. Computer lab courses teach how to work with a team to solve problems and complete assignments—something that you will probably do in this field—especially in the consulting business. Programming requires an understanding of mathematics and algorithms. Law enforcement classes are also beneficial. By learning the mindset of the criminal, you can better protect your client or employer. Last, being versed in intellectual property laws is important because you will be working with transmitting and protecting sensitive information as it travels to various locations.

Internships are the best way to gain hands-on experience. They offer real-life situations and protected work environments where you can see what Internet security is all about. Internships are not common, however, mostly because of security problems that arise from bringing inexperienced young people into contact with sensitive, confidential information. The majority of exposed hackers are under 20 years of age so it is easy to understand companies' unwillingness to offer internships.

On-the-job training is the best way to break into Internet security. Without experience, you can never land a job in the field.

Certification or Licensing

The International Webmasters Association offers a voluntary certification program for Internet security specialists and analysts. Certification is also available from various vendors of Internet security software and other products. Each vendor offers its own training and certification program, which varies from company to company. Some certifications can be completed in a matter of a few days; others take years. The majority of those employed in the field are not certified; however, certification is a trend and is considered an advantage. The more certifications you have, the more you have to offer a company.

The Internet is constantly evolving, and Internet technology changes so rapidly that it is vital for the Internet security specialist to stay on top of current technology. After all, if a hacker has knowledge of cutting edge technology and can use it to break into a system, the security specialist must be trained to counter those attacks. Security specialists must be well versed in the same cutting edge technology. Often, the vendor creating the most current technology is the best training source. In the future, the technology is likely to become more complex, and so is the training. Ideally, product certification coupled with a few years of hands-on experience qualifies you for advancement.

Other Requirements

If you like doing the same thing on a daily basis (like monitoring network activity logs and writing code), a job as Internet security specialist might be good for you. On the other hand, you must be flexible so that you are ready to meet each new challenge with fresh ideas. Some hackers are creative, and it is important that the security specialist be just as creative.

It is not uncommon for those applying for security positions to have background checks or at least have their list of references closely interviewed to make sure the applicants are trustworthy individuals. In fact, many companies prefer to hire individuals who have been recommended to them directly by someone they know and trust.

Consultants must be well organized because they work with many accounts at once. Communication skills are important because consultants often deal with management and try to sell them on the importance of security software. They must also be willing to travel on a regular basis to visit their accounts.

EXPLORING

If Internet security interests you, play around on your computer. Check out programming books from the local library and learn how to write simple code. You might also want to read professional publications such as Computer Security ALERT, which is published by the Computer Security Institute (http://www.gocsi.com/awareness/newsletters.jhtml), and *Information Security Magazine*, which is published by TechTarget (http://informationsecurity.techtarget. com). Another publication to consider is the quarterly magazine 2600 (http://www.2600.com). While 2600 is aimed at hackers, reading the articles will give you an understanding of how some systems are broken into and help you develop your ability to think of defenses.

Type of Security Technologies Used

The Computer Security Institute, in cooperation with the San Francisco office of the Federal Bureau of Investigation, conducts an annual survey of security practitioners in U.S. corporations, government agencies, universities, medical institutions, and financial institutions. Security practitioners reported using the security technologies listed in the following table.

Security Technology	Percentage of Security Practitioners Who Use It
Firewalls	97
Anti-virus software	96
Intrusion detection systems	72
Server-based access control lists	72
Encryption for data in transit	68
Reusable account/login passwords	52
Encrypted files	46
Smart cards/other one-time password tokens	42
Public key infrastructure	35
Intrusion prevention systems	35
Biometrics	15

Source: 2005 CSI/FBI Computer Crime & Security Survey, Computer Security Institute

High school science clubs and competitions will allow you to experiment with computer programming. They are great places to design and implement systems and solutions in a nonthreatening atmosphere. You can also work with other students to get accustomed to working in teams.

The most obvious place to learn about the Internet is on the Internet. Surf the Web and research the many security issues facing users today. Visit the sites of consulting firms where you can get an idea of the services these firms offer.

National news magazines, newspapers, and trade magazines are good sources of information. You can also find out a lot about current trends and hiring practices. Classified sections reveal what kind of market there is for security specialists and where the jobs are.

EMPLOYERS

Any company with an Internet presence (website, FTP site, email service, etc.) has the potential for security breaches and can benefit from the work and advice of an Internet security specialist. Depending on the size of the company and the nature of the company's business, it might use outside consultants or employ one part-time or several full-time employees.

An obvious place of employment is an Internet security consulting firm. Some business consulting firms like Ernst & Young are adding Internet security branches to their current businesses.

Data forensics is another growing business where Internet security specialists are hired to act as detectives to find culprits who break into computer networks. To fight this type of crime, the Federal Bureau of Investigation has set up a National Infrastructure Protection Center at its headquarters and Regional Computer Intrusion Squads in selected field offices throughout the United States.

STARTING OUT

It is unlikely that someone fresh out of high school or college will get a job as an Internet security specialist. Although education is important, experience is key in the field. Certifications are beneficial, but again, they do not mean much without experience. An internship in systems administration or engineering might introduce you to the security issues of that company.

Many who are in Internet security began in PC technical support and moved to systems administration or engineering. These jobs often include security responsibilities that then lead to positions focusing primarily on security.

If word-of-mouth doesn't get you a job, check the classifieds—both in the local newspapers and trade magazines. Many places post job openings on their websites.

ADVANCEMENT

Internet security specialists can move into supervisory or management positions and sometimes into executive positions. Those who work for small companies can sometimes advance by moving to larger firms with more sensitive data and more complicated security issues. With experience, an Internet security specialist can become a consultant.

Internet security consultants can become *sneakers* or part of a *tiger team*. Sneakers and tiger teams are the best in the field who are called in to crack a system on purpose in order to find security holes and then patch them.

EARNINGS

The field of Internet security is a lucrative business and the salary potential is growing. Internet security specialists are among the highest paid of all information technology professionals. An entry-level specialist can expect to earn $40,000 to $50,000. According to *Computerworld*'s 2005 Salary Survey, Internet security specialists had average salaries of $74,645 in 2005. They also received an average bonus of $6,390, which increases their total salary to $81,035.

Salaries increase with the size of the company and the nature of the information that specialists are charged with protecting. Specialists working with extremely confidential information in an industry (such as the automotive industry) will receive higher pay than those working at a small family business. The highest paying industries are manufacturing, computers, and communication/utilities companies. Military and government sectors pay the least.

Benefits for full-time employees may include paid vacation, paid sick days, personal days, medical and dental insurance, and bonuses.

WORK ENVIRONMENT

Because Internet security specialists work with computers and computers require a controlled atmosphere, the work environment is typically indoors in a well-lit, climate-controlled office. Security specialists can expect many hours of sitting in front of a computer screen using a keyboard. Work is generally done alone, although a consultant might train an in-house person on how to use certain software.

Most work schedules require 40 to 50 hours a week. Consultants travel frequently, and their work schedules do not necessarily follow typical nine-to-five working hours. There are instances where additional hours are required—for example, if a serious breach of security is detected and time is of the essence to fix it. It is not uncommon for employees to be on call so they can respond quickly to critical situations.

Although this line of work might seem stressful, it generally is not. Most businesses see the value of protecting their information and budget appropriately for the necessary tools, equipment, and staff.

OUTLOOK

Employment for Internet security specialists will grow faster than the average for all other occupations. The number of companies with a presence on the Internet is growing rapidly. As these companies connect their private networks to the public Internet, they will need to protect their confidential information. Currently, the demand for Internet security specialists is greater than the supply, and this trend is expected to continue as the number of businesses connecting to the Internet continues to grow.

Until now, most Internet security specialists have gotten by with general skills. In the future, however, they will need more specialized skills and certification. Staying on top of current technologies will be one of the biggest challenges.

Because of the ever-changing new technology, educational institutions will continue to have difficulty in training students for this field. Vendors and on-the-job experience will continue to provide the best training.

FOR MORE INFORMATION

A federally funded organization, the CERT Coordination Center studies, monitors, and publishes security-related activity and research. They also provide an incident response service to those who have been hacked.
CERT Coordination Center
Software Engineering Institute
Carnegie Mellon University
Pittsburgh, PA 15213-3890
Tel: 412-268-7090
Email: cert@cert.org
http://www.cert.org

A professional organization for information security professionals, CSI provides education and training for its members.
Computer Security Institute (CSI)
600 Harrison Street
San Francisco, CA 94107
Tel: 415-947-6320

Email: csi@cmp.com
http://www.gocsi.com

Information Security Magazine *is published by Tech Target and is a trade magazine for the information security professional.*
Information Security Magazine
117 Kendrick Street, Suite 800
Needham, MA 02494
Tel: 888-804-5501
http://informationsecurity.techtarget.com

For information on certification, contact the following organization:
International Webmasters Association
119 East Union Street, Suite F
Pasadena, CA 91103
Tel: 626-449-3709
http://www.iwanet.org

Internet Store Managers and Entrepreneurs

QUICK FACTS

School Subjects
Business
Computer science

Personal Skills
Leadership/management
Technical/scientific

Work Environment
Primarily indoors
Primarily one location

Minimum Education Level
Bachelor's degree

Salary Range
$25,000 to $50,000 to
$100,000

Certification or Licensing
Voluntary (certification)
Required by certain states
(licensing)

Outlook
Faster than the average

DOT
N/A

GOE
N/A

NOC
N/A

O*NET-SOC
N/A

OVERVIEW

Internet store managers and entrepreneurs use Internet technology to sell products or services. They may research the marketability of a product or service, decide on what product or service to sell, organize their business, and set up their storefront on the Web. Numerous small businesses owners who sell a limited number of products or a specific service have found the Internet a great place to begin their business venture because start-up costs may be less than for traditional businesses. Internet entrepreneurs run their own businesses. Internet store managers are employed by Internet entrepreneurs and stores.

HISTORY

The Internet became a popular sales tool in the 1990s and continues to grow today. Although many dot-com companies failed in the early 2000s, Internet sales remain an integral part of the U.S. economy.

In 2002, lawmakers and tax officials from 30 states agreed to enter a voluntary pact to collect online sales tax. According to washingtonpost.com, this action was taken partially in response to regular "bricks-and-mortar" stores that complained that online retailers had an advantage.

More and more revenue is generated online each year, and some Internet stores, such as Amazon.com, have had tremendous success in this field. As the Internet continues to grow in popularity and importance, more consumers will be exposed to Internet stores on a daily basis. This will create a strong demand for Internet managers and entrepreneurs to research and market potential products and services, as well as manage businesses and employees.

THE JOB

In spite of the failure of many high-profile dot-coms in the early 2000s, many online businesses have continued to survive and thrive. These e-tailers have adapted to the constantly changing technology, economic climate, business trends, and consumer demands, instead of concentrating on fast growth and offering the lowest prices. Reports by research firm Jupiter Communications show that consumers are using Internet stores to do comparison shopping, and a significant number of consumers research products online before buying them at traditional stores.

Because of the vastness of the Internet, the role of an Internet store manager or entrepreneur can vary as much as the numerous websites on the Internet. Expert opinion on what makes one website or one business more successful than another differs, too. E-commerce is a new and relatively unexplored field for entrepreneurs. But, because most entrepreneurs have innovative and creative natures, this uncertainty and uncharted territory is what they love.

Like traditional entrepreneurs, Internet entrepreneurs must have strong business skills. They come up with ideas for an Internet product or service, research the feasibility of selling this product or service, decide what they need to charge to make a profit, determine how to advertise their business, and even arrange for financing for their business if necessary. In addition, Internet entrepreneurs typically have computer savvy and may even create and maintain their own sites.

Some entrepreneurs may choose to market a service, such as website design, to target the business-to-business market. Other Internet entrepreneurs may decide to market a service, such as computer dating, to target the individual consumer market. Still others may develop a "virtual store" on the Internet and sell products that target businesses or individual consumers.

Internet stores vary in size, items for sale, and the range of products. Smaller Internet stores, for example, may market the work done by a single craftsperson or businessperson. Many large Internet stores focus on selling a specific product or line of products. As some of these stores have grown they have diversified their merchandise.

Amazon.com is one such example. Originally a small, online bookstore, the company now sells music CDs, videos, jewelry, toys and housewares, along with books. Other Internet stores, such as those of Eddie Bauer and Sears, may be extensions of catalog or traditional brick-and-mortar stores. These large companies are generally so well established that they can employ Internet store managers to oversee the virtual store.

Many Internet businesses begin small, with one person working as the owner, manager, webmaster, marketing director, and accountant, among other positions. John Axne of Chicago, Illinois, took on all these responsibilities when he developed his own one-person business designing websites for small companies and corporations. "Having my own business allows me more creative freedom," says Axne. The successful Internet entrepreneur, like the successful traditional entrepreneur, is often able to combine his or her interests with work to fill a niche in the business world. "It's a great fit for me," Axne explains. "I have a passion for computers and a love of learning. This business allows me to sell myself and my services." Dave Wright of Venice, California, is also an Internet entrepreneur and website designer. He, too, combined his interests with computer skills to start his business. "I had a strong interest in art," he says. "I simply married my art and graphic art experience with computers."

Those who want to start their own businesses on the Web must be very focused and self-motivated. Just like any other entrepreneur, they always need to keep an eye on the competition to see what products and services as well as prices and delivery times others offer. While Internet entrepreneurs do not need to be computer whizzes, they should enjoy learning about technology so that they can keep up with new developments that may help them with their businesses. Internet entrepreneurs must also be decision makers, and many are drawn to running their own businesses because of the control it offers. "I'm a control freak," Wright admits. "This way I can oversee every aspect of my job."

The typical day of the Internet store manager or entrepreneur will depend greatly on the company he or she works for. Someone who works for a large company that also has a website store, for example, may meet with company department heads to find out about upcoming sales or products that should be heavily advertised on the website. They may do research about the store use and report their findings to company managers. They may work on the site itself, updating it with new information.

The Internet entrepreneur also has varied responsibilities that depend on his or her business. Wright notes, "No two projects and

Jeff Bezos, founder and CEO of Amazon.com, speaks to reporters at a press conference. *(Landov)*

no two days are alike." An entrepreneur may spend one day working with a client to determine the client's needs and the next day working on bookkeeping and advertising in addition to working on a project. Most entrepreneurs, however, enjoy this variety and flexibility.

While the Internet world is appealing to many, there are risks for those who start their own businesses. "The Internet changes so rapidly that in five years it may be entirely different," Wright says. "That's why I started a business that simply sells services and didn't require a major investment. It is a business that I can get into and out of quickly if I find it necessary. There is no product, per se, and no inventory." Despite uncertainties, however, Web stores continue to open and the number of Internet store managers and entrepreneurs continues to grow.

REQUIREMENTS

High School

If you are considering becoming an Internet store manager or entrepreneur, there are a number of classes you can take in high school to help prepare you for these careers. Naturally you should take computer science courses to become familiar with using computers and the Web. Business and marketing courses will also be beneficial for you. Also, take mathematics, accounting, or bookkeeping classes because, as an entrepreneur, you will be responsible for your company's finances. Take history classes to learn about economic trends and psychology classes to learn about human behavior. A lot of advertising and product promotion has a psychological element. Finally, take plenty of English classes. These classes will help you develop your communication skills—skills that will be vital to your work as a store manager or business owner.

Postsecondary Training

Although there are no specific educational requirements for Internet store managers or entrepreneurs, a college education will certainly enhance your skills and chances for success. Like anyone interested in working for or running a traditional business, take plenty of business, economics, and marketing and management classes. Your education should also include accounting or bookkeeping classes. Keep up with computer and Internet developments by taking computer classes. Some schools offer classes on e-commerce. Many schools have undergraduate degree programs in business or business administration, but you can also enter this field with other degrees. Dave Wright, for example, graduated with a degree from art school, while John Axne has degrees in biomedical engineering and interactive media.

Certification or Licensing

Professional associations such as the Institute for Certification of Computing Professionals, the Institute of Certified Professional Managers, and the International Webmasters Association offer voluntary management-related certifications to industry professionals. These designations are helpful in proving your abilities to an employer. The more certifications you have, the more you have to offer.

Licenses may be required for running a business, depending on the type of business. Since requirements vary, you will need to check with local and state agencies for regulations in your area.

Other Requirements

Internet entrepreneurs and store managers must have the desire and initiative to keep up on new technology and business trends. Because they must deal with many different people in various lines of work, they need to be flexible problem solvers and have strong communication skills. Creativity and insight into new and different ways of doing business are qualities that are essential for an entrepreneur to be successful. In addition, because the Internet and e-commerce are relatively new and the future of Internet businesses is uncertain, those who enter the field are generally risk-takers and eager to be on the cutting edge of commerce and technology. Dave Wright notes, "This is not a job for someone looking for security. The Internet world is always changing. This is both exciting and scary to me as a businessperson. This is one career where you are not able to see where you will be in five years."

EXPLORING

There are numerous ways in which you can explore your interest in the computer and business worlds. Increase your computer skills and find out how much this technology interests you by joining a computer users group or club at your high school or in your community. Access the Internet frequently on your own to observe different website designs and find out what is being sold and marketed electronically. What sites do you think are best at promoting products and why? Think about things from a customer's point of view. How easy are the sites to access and use? How are the products displayed and accessed? How competitive are the prices for goods or services?

Make it a goal to come up with your own ideas for a product or service to market on the Web, then do some research. How difficult would it be to deliver the product? What type of financing would be involved? Are there other sites already providing this product or service? How could you make your business unique?

Talk to professionals in your community about their work. Set up informational interviews with local business owners to find out what is involved in starting and running a traditional business. Your local chamber of commerce or the Small Business Administration may have classes or publications that would help you learn about starting a business. In addition, set up informational interviews with computer consultants, website designers, or Internet store managers or owners. How did they get started? What advice do they have? Is there anything they wish they had done differently? Where do they see the future of e-commerce going?

If your school has a future business owners club, join this group to meet others with similar interests. For hands-on business experience, get a part-time or summer job at any type of store in your area. This work will give you the opportunity to deal with customers (who can sometimes be hard to please), work with handling money, and observe how the store promotes its products and services.

EMPLOYERS

Internet store managers may work for an established traditional business or institution that also has a website dealing with products and services. The manager may also work for a business that only has a presence on the Web or for an Internet entrepreneur. Entrepreneurs are self-employed, and sometimes they may employ people to work under them. Some Internet entrepreneurs may be hired to begin a business for someone else.

STARTING OUT

Professionals in the field advise those just starting out to work for someone else to gain experience in the business world before beginning their own business. The Internet is a good resource to use to find employment. There are many sites that post job openings. Local employment agencies and newspapers and trade magazines also list job opportunities. In addition, your college career services office should be able to provide you with help locating a job. Networking with college alumni and people in your computer users groups may also provide job leads.

ADVANCEMENT

Advancement opportunities depend on the business, its success, and the individual's goals. Internet entrepreneurs or store managers who are successful may enter other business fields or consulting. Or they may advance to higher-level management positions or other larger Internet-based businesses. Some entrepreneurs establish a business and then sell it only to begin another business venture. The Internet world is constantly changing because of technological advancements. This state of flux means that a wide variety of possibilities are available to those working in the field. "There is no solid career path in the Internet field," says Dave Wright. "Your next career may not even be developed yet."

EARNINGS

Income for Internet store managers and entrepreneurs is usually tied to the profitability of the business. Internet store managers who work for established traditional businesses are typically salaried employees of the company. Internet entrepreneurs who offer a service may be paid by the project. Entrepreneurs are self-employed and their income will depend on the success of the business. Those just starting out may actually have no earnings, while those with a business that has been in existence for several years may have annual earnings between $25,000 and $50,000. Some in the field may earn much more than this amount. John Axne estimates that those who have good technical skills and can do such things as create the database program for a website may have higher salaries, in the $60,000 to $125,000 range.

Entrepreneurs are almost always responsible for their own medical, disability, and life insurances. Retirement plans must also be self-funded and self-directed. Internet store managers may or may not receive benefits.

WORK ENVIRONMENT

Internet entrepreneurs and store managers may work out of a home or private office. Some Internet store managers may be required to work on site at a corporation or small business.

The entrepreneur must deal with the stresses of starting a business, keeping it going, dealing with deadlines and customers, and coping with problems as they arise. They must also work long hours to develop and manage their business venture; many entrepreneurs work over 40 hours a week. Evening or weekend work may also be required, both for the entrepreneur and the store manager.

In addition, these professionals must spend time researching, reading, and checking out the competition in order to be informed about the latest technology and business trends. Their intensive computer work can result in eyestrain, hand and wrist injuries, and back pain.

OUTLOOK

Online commerce is a very new and exciting field with tremendous potential, and it is likely that growth will continue over the long term. However, it is important to keep in mind that the failure rate for new businesses, even traditional ones, is fairly high. Some experts predict that in the next few years, 80 to 90 percent of dot-coms will either close or be acquired by other companies. The survivors will be small businesses that are able to find niche markets, anticipate trends, adapt to market and technology changes, and plan for a large enough financial margin to turn a profit. Analysts also anticipate that the amount of business-to-business e-commerce will surpass business-to-consumer sales.

Internet managers and entrepreneurs with the most thorough education and experience and who have done their research will have the best opportunities for success. For those who are adventurous and interested in using new avenues for selling products and services, the Internet offers many possibilities.

FOR MORE INFORMATION

For certification information, contact
Institute for Certification of Computing Professionals
2350 East Devon Avenue, Suite 115
Des Plaines, IL 60018-4610
Tel: 800-843-8227
Email: office@iccp.org
http://www.iccp.org

For information on certification, contact
Institute of Certified Professional Managers
James Madison University
MSC 5504
Harrisonburg, VA 22807
Tel: 800-568-4120
Email: icpmcm@jmu.edu
http://cob.jmu.edu/icpm

For information on certification, contact the following organization:
International Webmasters Association
119 East Union Street, Suite F
Pasadena, CA 91103
Tel: 626-449-3709
http://www.iwanet.org

The Small Business Administration offers helpful information on starting a business.
Small Business Administration
409 Third Street, SW
Washington, DC 20416
Tel: 800-827-5722
Email: answerdesk@sba.gov
http://www.sba.gov

Internet Transaction Specialists

OVERVIEW

Depending on their level of expertise, *Internet transaction specialists* may be in charge of designing, developing, or implementing Internet transaction software or systems. This software or system is the technology that allows a customer to buy a book online, for example, by giving his or her credit card number. Internet transaction specialists at the most advanced professional level are often called *architects,* and they oversee the design of the whole transaction system. They decide what direction a system should take and what technology should be used. *Software developers* work under the guidance of architects to turn these designs into reality. Less experienced programmers may also contribute by working on smaller parts of the program that the developer or architect assigns them.

HISTORY

Since the boom of the World Wide Web in the 1990s, companies have flocked to use Internet technology to communicate with employees, customers, clients, buyers, and future stockholders. As a result, these companies need workers to ensure that their systems are secure, and to develop improved systems so that transactions can take place more quickly.

At first, the majority of Internet sites were created and maintained by a sole individual who was a jack-of-all-trades. Today, websites are often designed, implemented, and managed by entire departments composed of numerous individuals, such as Internet transaction specialists, who specialize in creating the systems or software used to conduct transactions on the Internet.

As consumers become more comfortable with buying online and companies expand their Internet businesses, Internet transaction specialists will be needed to ensure that systems are running smoothly and efficiently.

THE JOB

Every business engaged in e-commerce must use some type of Internet transaction software, that is, software that allows money to be transferred from the customer to the business. This process is also referred to as *electronic funds transfer* (*EFT*). Transaction software and systems are what allow customers to do such things as transfer funds between banks, pay bills online, and buy and sell stocks. At the same time, transaction software and systems are what allow businesses to get credit card approval for a customer's purchase, receive payments, and make money transfers. As e-commerce has become more and more popular, the need for Internet transaction specialists has grown. In addition, the technology itself continues to develop. According to Gene Krause, president and director of sales and marketing of Intellefunds Inc., in St. Louis, Missouri, "Electronic funds transfer is continually evolving. It is getting better and more efficient and is revolutionizing Internet transactions."

One of the major responsibilities of an Internet transaction specialist is to ensure the security of a system. Because these transactions involve money and because they take place over the Internet, the possibility exists for online theft. Customers need to feel sure that when they buy shoes or groceries online, for example, their credit card numbers won't be stolen or their bank accounts emptied by hackers breaking into the system. Transaction specialists constantly work to improve protocols for secure financial transactions. Jeff Thorness, of ACH Direct in Cathedral City, California, an EFT company, is his company's primary programmer as well as chief executive officer. Security is one of his top concerns. "Our software is very sophisticated and secure," he explains. "We can quickly deal with problems where the purchase may be over the credit limit or where fraud is suspected. Our software can analyze transactions immediately."

Another major responsibility of the specialist is to improve software and systems so that transactions are speedier and less complicated, allowing banks, credit card companies, and stores selling goods online to exchange financial data more rapidly and directly than ever before. Improvements also provide customers greater access to goods and services. Through EFT, for example, customers may be able to transfer funds from a bank account directly to a business. Thorness explains, "Electronic funds transfer even allows the consumer who has no credit cards to purchase products online." He says that this is also good for the business because, "It enables a larger Internet client base."

Some companies have large enough e-commerce needs that they have their own in-house Internet architects, developers, and programmers designing and implementing transaction systems. Other smaller companies may hire a firm specializing in e-commerce systems to perform this service. Some firms specializing in transaction software simply implement that software for companies developing or improving their e-commerce sites. On the cutting edge are firms working to push transaction software standards forward, developing new ways to perform transactions online.

Thorness is an in-house specialist and his days include a variety of activities. "On any given day, I may oversee the mechanical applications of the software and website, support the reseller, solve technical problems, and deal with customer service issues. Plus," he adds, "I must oversee the total operations side where we receive transactions that flow through our system to the Federal Reserve System." In-house specialists, as well as outside specialists who are hired by a company to work on a project, must have excellent communication skills. They meet with management to find out what services the company wants to offer its customers through the Internet and determine what type of programming is needed. Often the specialists will work with other programmers to build the software and system. In addition, specialists must be able to deal with the frustration that comes when programming does not work as they had anticipated. Tight deadlines can also make the job of the transaction specialist fairly stressful.

Despite the stress and frustration that are part of this work, many people find this job rewarding. "When you develop programs you get a sense of accomplishment throughout the job. You are actually building a product or service," Thorness says. He also sees a bright future for transaction specialists. "There are lots of career opportunities on various levels," Thorness notes. "We are in the midst of a computer revolution. Business people are talking to each other in similar languages. Transactions such as billing and bill payment over the Internet are just beginning."

REQUIREMENTS

High School

There are a number of classes you can take in high school to help get ready for this career. Improving your computer skills should be a priority; therefore, take as many computer classes as possible. Develop your analytical and problem-solving skills by taking mathematics classes such as algebra, geometry, and precalculus, and science classes, such as chemistry and physics. To get an idea of how companies function, take business and economics classes. English classes are essential and will help you develop your communication, research, and writing skills.

Postsecondary Training

In the early days of Internet and computer development, many people without college degrees were able to find jobs in the field if they had computer experience. Jeff Thorness developed his computer skills at an early age. "I was one of those lucky people who grew up understanding computers," he says. "By the time I got out of high school I knew more than they could teach me in college. I was already developing, programming, and designing complex software." However, as this field has matured and the market has grown tighter, many companies now require new hires to have college degrees. In addition, a college degree may help you to advance professionally. Typically, people entering this field have degrees in computer science; some have degrees in other areas such as computer engineering, business, or mathematics. The most important aspect of your education, however, is to gain a thorough knowledge of computers and programming. It will be to your benefit to complete an internship or do summer work in programming at a computer company or a company with a computer/technology division. When you are deciding on a college to attend, find out if its career services office has information on such internships or jobs.

People working in some advanced positions, such as architect, may be required to have extensive computer and business experience as well as an undergraduate or graduate degree.

Certification or Licensing

There are numerous certifications available in programming languages, software, and network administration. Some employers may require that you have certain certifications although most employers are more interested in your skills and experience. Nevertheless, certification will enhance your professional standing and show your commitment to the field. The certification process usually involves taking a training program and passing a written exam.

Other Requirements

You should enjoy learning about new technology and be able to learn on your own as well as through organized classes. People in this field constantly improve their skills by reading about the latest developments and teaching themselves new techniques. You'll need the desire and initiative to keep up on new technology, software, and hardware. You must also have good verbal and written communication skills because you will often have to communicate with a team or with the end user.

Jeff Thorness states, "You must be a logical thinker and a hard worker. You must be able to concentrate for long periods of time and be persistent in finding a problem and finishing a project." You must be able to work under stressful situations, such as meeting important deadlines, and deal with frustration when the programming is not working the way you had planned. Because you will deal with many different problems you must be flexible and patient.

Depending on what area you want to specialize in, you may need good customer service skills or design ability. "If you are getting into the tech support area," Thorness says, "you must analyze and dissect the problem and have the ability to deal with all issues. You need to be helpful and have good customer service skills." He adds, "If you want to get into the Web design aspect you should have database and design skills. Again, the ability to think logically is important."

How Many People Are Online?

World: 605.60 million

Europe: 190.91 million

Asia/Pacific: 187.24 million

U.S. and Canada: 182.67 million

Latin America: 33.35 million

Africa: 6.31 million

Middle East: 5.12 million

Source: Nua Internet Surveys, September 2002

EXPLORING

One of the best ways to explore this field is to get hands-on experience working with computers. "Get a job at a computer store and get 'hands-on dirty' with the hardware issues," suggests Jeff Thorness. "Get real-world experience by getting into programming. Buy books and experiment with Web development tools." Join your high school computer users group or start one of your own. You may be able to learn about new technology developments from others in your group.

In addition to reading books on programming, look at computer magazines for the latest news. Some publications, such as the quarterly magazine *2600* (http://www.2600.com), have articles about security issues. While *2600* is aimed at hackers, reading the articles will give you an understanding of how some systems are broken into and help you develop your ability to think of defenses.

Naturally, you should use computers and the Web as often as you can. If a community center or tech school in your area offers computer classes that are more advanced than those offered at your high school, be sure to take them. Also, your computer teacher or school guidance counselor may be able to help you contact professionals in the field and set up informational interviews with them. Even if you can't find an Internet transaction specialist to interview, talking with anyone in the field, such as programmers, website designers, or consultants, will give you an idea of what computer work is like.

EMPLOYERS

Internet transaction specialists may work in-house, as salaried employees of companies such as those with an Internet presence, those that develop software and provide electronic funds transfer services, or financial institutions. Others may work for firms that specialize in developing the transaction software and systems for companies without an in-house transaction staff. These companies hire the firms to build or improve their Internet sites.

Job opportunities are available worldwide; however, major cities with a high concentration of Internet, technology, and software companies may provide the best opportunities.

STARTING OUT

Many transaction specialists begin their careers working as junior programmers under the supervision of more experienced developers and architects. Only after they prove their skills and work ethic on the job are beginning programmers considered for positions with greater responsibility.

Apply for employment directly to consulting firms, Internet and software companies, as well as corporations, businesses, and financial institutions that have in-house computer divisions. Classified ads, employment agencies, and Internet job listings can also provide some possible job leads. Your college career services office should also be able to help you locate a position. Networking with others in the computer industry and the community is a good way to make the contacts that may lead to employment. To network, get in touch with previous business associates, computer user groups, and trade organizations. In addition, your college internship or summer work with computers may provide you with contacts and job leads. A willingness to learn and to work hard is the key to a good start as well as advancement in the computer industry.

ADVANCEMENT

Specialists who have advanced through the ranks of junior programmers to senior architects can take their careers in any of a number of directions. Those with project management skills may move up to executive managerial or supervisory positions that require more planning than programming. Persons with excellent programming and development skills may become involved in more cutting-edge programming work, like developing standards for Internet transactions.

Continued learning, certifications, and degrees may provide the specialist with a competitive edge when it comes to advancing within the industry.

EARNINGS

Earnings for transaction specialists vary and depend on factors such as a person's experience, knowledge, and geographic location as well as the size of the company he or she works for. Salaries for junior programmers without much experience usually begin around $45,000 annually. On the other end of the scale, senior software architects can earn as much as $200,000, though salaries between $75,000 and $100,000 are more common. Developers and mid-range programmers tend to fall in the middle of these two—closer to one or the other depending on their years of experience and the size of the firm. According to *Computerworld*'s *2005 Salary Survey*, network architects earned average annual salaries of $86,039 in 2005. They also received an average bonus of $8,161, which increased their total salary to $94,200.

As with other Internet-related jobs, hourly wage figures tend to be higher for programmers working as consultants.

Typical benefits for full-time employees include health, life, and disability insurance; sick leave; and vacation pay. Retirement plans may also be available, and some companies may match employees' contributions. Some companies may also offer stock-option plans. In a highly competitive market, companies may offer a sign-on bonus to a new, talented employee.

WORK ENVIRONMENT

Internet transaction specialists can generally expect to work in a clean, comfortable office environment. The office atmosphere may vary greatly depending on the company. Those working in large, traditional businesses, such as banks, will generally experience a more formal and structured environment.

The job of the transaction specialist can be frustrating and stressful, and frequently long hours are required to finish a project. Many people in the computer field often work more than 40 hours a week and are required to work nights and weekends. Jeff Thorness notes that it is common for him to work 12 hours a day, six days a week. "When we are in the middle of designing a new system and the hours become critical, it can be more," he says. In addition, Internet transaction specialists who are dedicated to keeping up with technology and the Internet community must spend a considerable amount of their free time reading, researching, and keeping abreast of computer and Internet technologies.

To guard against eyestrain, back pain, and hand and wrist injuries that can come from intensive computer work, Internet transaction specialists must use good equipment such as ergonomic chairs and keyboards.

OUTLOOK

The future of transaction specialists will be closely tied to the future of e-commerce itself. In the beginnings of e-commerce, there was extremely rapid growth for a number of high-profile successful companies. During the early 2000s, however, many of these businesses failed or were taken over by other companies, and there was a wave of layoffs and firings. Studies have shown that these companies offered large discounts to attract customers and failed to plan for a large enough financial margin to turn a profit. Many smaller businesses have pulled through the dot-com crisis because they concentrated on a niche market, provided products and services targeted to their specific demands, and paid careful attention to the bottom line.

Experts predict a turnaround for dot-com businesses in the next few years, but job security with any one firm may be uncertain. Mergers, business failures, downsizing, and the ever-changing technology of this industry mean that there may be some instability regarding long-term employment with any one firm. Nevertheless, those who keep current with technology and are always willing to learn and adapt will be in high demand.

Gene Krause sees growth possibilities for the industries involving EFT. "Electronic funds transfer is continually evolving. It is getting better and more efficient. It is revolutionizing Internet transactions. We are getting to the real-time payment method that is friendly and secure," he says. Krause also predicts growth in other areas, "Electronic bill payment will also increase and it will all be Internet based. Transactions will be speedier and costs will be reduced. Transactions through bank accounts will increase." The potential advantages of secure online transactions, especially increased speed and accuracy in business-to-business communications, should continue to fuel the development of this technology for years to come. Naturally, skilled transaction specialists will be needed to make these developments possible.

FOR MORE INFORMATION

This center studies Internet security problems and provides security alerts. For industry news, check out its website.
CERT Coordination Center
Software Engineering Institute
Carnegie Mellon University
Pittsburgh, PA 15213-3890
Tel: 412-268-7090
Email: cert@cert.org
http://www.cert.org

For information on the industry, conferences, and seminars, contact
Computer Security Institute
600 Harrison Street
San Francisco, CA 94107
Tel: 415-947-6320
Email: csi@cmp.com
http://www.gocsi.com

Online Journalists

QUICK FACTS

School Subjects
Computer science
English

Personal Skills
Communication/ideas
Technical/scientific

Work Environment
Primarily indoors
Primarily one location

Minimum Education Level
Bachelor's degree

Salary Range
$18,340 to $38,707 to
$79,227

Certification or Licensing
None available

Outlook
Faster than the average

DOT
131

GOE
01.03.01

NOC
5123

O*NET-SOC
27-3022.00

OVERVIEW

Online journalists research and write content for Internet websites. They may be full-time salaried workers or employed on a freelance basis. They may work for online publications, professional associations, businesses with an online presence, or the government. Some writers are volunteer online columnists or contributors and do not get paid for their writing.

HISTORY

One of the greatest things about the World Wide Web is that people can gain access to information from around the world with a click of a mouse. Whether one wants to know about international news, current events, fitness trends, or recipes, the Internet has a wealth of information on the topic. This would not be possible without the work of writers such as online journalists.

As newspapers, journals, businesses, and organizations continue to make their presence known on the Internet, job opportunities will continue to open up for writers to create, edit, and update the content of sites. The popularity of news sites such as *The Wall Street Journal Online* (http://www.wsj.com) and CNN.com (http://www.cnn.com) prove that their is a market for dependable, timely online news outlets.

THE JOB

The work of online journalists is published on websites in online publications. They may write articles for "e-zines" (online magazines), press releases that are posted on company or society websites, or stories for online newspapers. The online journalist must pay special attention to the tone and length of an article. Few readers will scroll through screen after screen of text.

"Writing for the Web is somewhat different than print journalism," says Maria Erspamer, an editorial director for a website and a freelance online journalist in Venice, California. "The attention span of online readers is not as great." Erspamer explains that the online journalist must be able to write in a style that provides news while also engaging the reader's interest. "You need to use a standard voice, meaning that there must be a mix of entertainment and information in your writing. Along with that you need to be concise, since many online readers scan the content."

While online journalists do not need to be computer geniuses, they do need to know what computer and Internet tools can make their articles more interesting. Frequently, online journalists incorporate highlighted key words, lists, pop-up boxes or windows, and hypertext links in their articles. These items make the articles visually appealing and easy to read. In addition, such things as hypertext links and pop-up windows allow the journalist to include a depth of information in articles that might otherwise be short and superficial.

Stacie Kilgore of Peachtree City, Georgia, is a senior analyst and online journalist for a major research and consulting firm. She believes that, in a sense, writing for the online audience is easier than writing for a print source. "I can include more information," she says. "For instance, in my articles I can include pop-up windows that explain a terminology or concept. This allows me to reach a wider audience. I can write for the more experienced audience and still be able to reach the newcomers or those with limited technical knowledge."

Online journalists work for publishing companies of various sizes. These companies may be businesses that have been built solely around Web journalism, such as the e-zine *Salon,* or they may be traditional publishing companies that have also developed a Web presence, such as the *New York Times* or *Entertainment Weekly.* Online journalists may also work for news organizations, research firms, and other businesses that have websites where articles are published. Some online journalists are full-time salaried employees of companies, while others may work on a freelance basis. As a freelancer, the online journalist runs his or her own business. The freelancer may get an assignment from a company to write a particular article, or the freelancer may write an article and then attempt to sell it to a company for publication.

Erspamer enjoys her freelance work because it allows her the opportunity to write about topics that interest her. "I always have ideas for articles," she says, "and the Internet offers a wealth of material and creative venues." When Erspamer writes an article that she hopes to sell to an online publishing company, she must research the topic, find out what other articles on the subject have already been published, decide on the marketability of her article idea, and write about the topic in a new and interesting way that will make her article stand out from others. Freelancers also need business skills to keep track of their financial accounts and market their work. Erspamer notes, "With freelancing it is sometimes difficult to retrieve payment for articles I have written. Sometimes I have to be a forceful business person as well as a journalist."

Both freelance and salaried online journalists must be organized and able to work under time pressures. The deadlines for online journalists can be similar to those for print journalists. Erspamer notes, "Some articles are time-sensitive, meaning that they must be written and disseminated quickly or the information will no longer be valuable." This time-sensitive factor is especially true for those working for news organizations. Deadlines will be tight, particularly since readers turn to websites expecting to find the most up-to-date information possible.

"I have to be very deadline conscious in my job," Erspamer says. When she receives assignments from online publishers, she reviews the articles to be written and prioritizes them according to the assigned deadlines. After she has completed this step, she says, "I do Internet research on the subject, seek out experts to interview to provide backup information, and then write the articles in the order of their importance and the deadlines." After the articles are written, they are reviewed and turned in to the publisher.

As an online editor, Erspamer solicits writers whose expertise matches the material she needs written. Her responsibilities include overseeing the project to its completion. "I manage the materials and make sure they are all written in the voice that speaks for our product and company," she says.

Many people working in online writing view the speed at which an article can go from the concept stage to the published stage as an asset. "I like being an online editor because I like being involved with creating a voice for the website, overseeing the written content, and seeing immediate feedback," Erspamer says.

Kilgore also takes satisfaction from publishing her writing online. "What I write gets dispersed quickly, yet it is archived,"

Arianna Huffington, online journalist and political activist, makes a point during a roundtable discussion. *(Landov)*

she says. "The article is long-standing, and readers can retrieve it quickly through a search, so essentially my articles live on forever."

One drawback to the online journalist's career is that many Internet companies are not well established, and thus job security is minimal. However, for those writers interested in being on the cutting edge of technology and having their writing available to millions, the online journalism field is the right place to be.

REQUIREMENTS

High School

If you are considering a career as an online journalist, you should take college preparatory classes while in high school. Concentrate on English classes that allow you to develop your research and writing skills. Take computer classes that teach you to use word processing programs, graphics, and the Internet. If your school offers journalism classes, take these to develop your news writing style and to learn about publications. To prepare for college and have the broad educational background any writer needs, take mathematics, science, and history classes.

Postsecondary Training

Many online journalists have bachelor's degrees in journalism. You may also be able to enter the field with a degree in English or communications. A number of universities have journalism programs in online journalism, sometimes known as new media.

In addition to your journalism studies, continue to take computer classes. Learning HTML, a website authoring language, can also be helpful to an online journalist and may qualify you for other writing and editing opportunities. It is also essential that you learn the most popular software programs and office tools that relate to the writing profession.

Finally, one of the most beneficial things you can do during your college years is to gain hands-on experience through a journalism internship or summer job at a publishing company. Working in online journalism, naturally, is best. But even if you have an internship at a traditional print publication, you will gain valuable experience. Some schools' career services offices or journalism departments have information on such internships.

Other Requirements

If you want to be an online journalist, you will need good research skills. You must have a love for learning and enjoy searching for new information. You must have the desire and initiative to keep up-to-date on new technology and the changes that are constantly taking place on the Internet. You must also have good communication skills and the ability to listen and interpret what others are saying. All journalists must have good grammar, spelling, and editing skills. Online journalists, in particular, must know how to write concisely. You must also be organized, self-motivated, and able to meet strict deadlines. Because you will deal with many different people in various lines of work, you must have good interpersonal skills.

EXPLORING

To explore the journalism aspect of this career while you are still in high school, join your school's newspaper staff. As a reporter, you will have the experience of researching, interviewing people, and writing articles on deadline. If you do layout work with the computer, you will gain experience using publishing software. Another way to explore your interest in writing is to join a local writing group. Your high school, local library, or community center may sponsor writing groups; in addition, these groups may be advertised in the local newspaper. Contact your local newspaper to arrange for an informational interview with a journalist there. If the newspaper has an online version, ask to speak with someone who works on the online publication. During the interview you'll have the opportunity to ask a professional what the best parts of their job are, what

Books to Read

Bass, Frank. *The Associated Press Guide to Internet Research and Reporting*. New York: Perseus Publishing, 2002.

Hall, Jim. *Online Journalism: A Critical Primer*. London, U.K.: Pluto Press, 2001.

Hammerich, Irene, and Claire Harrison. *Developing Online Content: The Principles of Writing and Editing for the Web*. Hoboken, N.J.: John Wiley & Sons, 2001.

Pavlik, John Vernon, and Seymour Topping. *Journalism and New Media*. New York: Columbia University Press, 2001.

Ward, Mike. *Journalism Online*. Burlington, Mass.: Focal Press, 2002.

type of education and experience he or she has, and other questions that interest you.

To explore the computer and Internet aspects of this career, surf the Web on a regular basis to check out sites and read their content. Join a computer users group at your school or in the area. If your high school has a website, volunteer to update the site periodically with reports on school news and events. You could also work on updating the information posted on the websites of other organizations you are involved with, such as your church, temple, or mosque.

If you have a particular interest in a subject or hobby, write some articles and submit them to an appropriate website for publication. Many websites do not pay for unsolicited material; however, getting an article published is an excellent way to break into the field and also to determine if an online journalism career is something you wish to pursue.

EMPLOYERS

Online journalists may work for publishing companies that only produce online publications, for traditional publishing companies that also have a Web presence, and for news organizations, research firms, or other businesses that have websites. Online journalists may also work as freelancers, writing articles for various companies and sites.

Companies involved in online publishing are located across the country; company sizes vary. While large and well-known companies such as the *New York Times* attract a large share of the online audience, the ease and affordability of online publishing is allowing many smaller companies to produce online publications.

STARTING OUT

To get started in this field, a budding journalist may want to write articles and attempt to get them published. According to Maria Erspamer, "The online market is more open to new, unpublished writers than traditional markets. Try to get published on these sites. Many online sites pay little or nothing for articles; however, they will usually provide clips of published work, which helps a new writer develop a portfolio and credibility."

Some online journalists believe that those interested in the career will benefit from starting out in print journalism and then transferring their skills to online journalism. Those starting out in either print journalism or online journalism usually begin in the position of editorial assistant. Although the editorial assistant job is relatively low paying, it will give you the opportunity to learn the business and usually provides you with your first writing assignments. Talented and hard-working assistants will typically work their way up to full-fledged reporters.

Your college career services office and journalism or communications department should be able to give you help with your job search. In addition, contacts that you make during an internship or summer job may provide employment leads. You can also apply for employment directly to publishing companies or other companies with Web publications. Use classified ads and the Internet as resources when looking for job openings.

ADVANCEMENT

Some journalists believe it is easier to move through the ranks as an online journalist than as a traditional journalist working for a newspaper, TV station, or radio station. One reason for this is that online journalism is a relatively new and growing field offering many opportunities. Advancement will also depend on an individual's goals. A salaried journalist may consider it an advancement to do freelance work full time. A full-time freelancer may advance by publishing more articles and expanding his or her client base. Other advancements may mean a shift in career focus away from journalism. Maria Erspamer explains, "There can be career transition or advancement from a writer to a content developer for a Web company." Another online advancement can be moving up to the position of *editor, communications director,* or *online producer.*

Some online journalists advance their careers by transferring to the print medium and working their way up the ranks of a newspaper or magazine.

EARNINGS

There are no official salary figures currently available for online journalists. However, as with other Web-related jobs, online journalists may make slightly higher salaries than their counterparts in traditional journalism. According to the U.S. Department of Labor, the median yearly income of traditional newspaper reporters was $31,660 in 2004. The lowest 10 percent of all reporters earned less than $18,340; the highest 10 percent earned more than $68,880. Online journalists generally earn salaries on the higher end of this scale. Salary.com reported that Web writers had salaries that ranged from less than $38,707 to $79,227 or more in 2004, depending on their level of expertise.

Incomes are influenced by such factors as the person's experience, company size, and geographic location. Freelance online journalists' hourly fees range from $25 to $125 depending on the project and the writer's experience.

Typical benefits may be available for full-time salaried employees, including sick leave, vacation pay, and health, life, and disability insurance. Retirement plans may also be available, and some companies may match employees' contributions. Some companies may also offer stock-option plans.

Freelance journalists do not receive benefits and are responsible for their own medical, disability, and life insurance. They do not receive vacation pay, and when they aren't working, they aren't generating income. Retirement plans must also be self-funded and self-directed.

WORK ENVIRONMENT

Online journalists may work in a variety of settings. Freelancers generally work out of their homes or private offices. Salaried writers working for a company generally work out of the company's offices in a clean, well-lit facility. Telecommuting is becoming more popular and may be an option at some companies. Whatever setting online journalists work in, they have access to technology equipment such as computers, modems, phones, and faxes.

Depending on the project, journalists may work independently or as part of a team of journalists. In addition, they frequently contact people outside of the journalism profession to interview for articles or information. Work hours may vary, and overtime may be needed to finish a project on deadline. Writing can be a frustrating job when articles do not come together as the writer had planned. The environment can be intense as journalists work to produce articles quickly while providing accurate and concise information.

Although publishing companies have traditionally had a business atmosphere, they are often more relaxed than other corporate environments. Many high-tech companies, especially smaller ones, also have a casual office atmosphere that promotes camaraderie and teamwork.

OUTLOOK

Though the overall employment rate for reporters is expected to grow slowly due to newspaper mergers, closures, decreased circulation, and more limited revenues, more rapid job growth is expected in new media areas, including online newspapers and magazines. The employment of online reporters should grow faster than the average for all occupations through the next decade. Traditional publishers and broadcasters have continued to move into Web publishing, indicating that online publishing will most likely continue to grow.

Online journalism will continue to evolve as journalists begin to devise new ways to take advantage of the interactivity offered by the Web. However, as the field becomes more established and the number of journalists who have online experience grows, competition for jobs is expected to become more intense.

The Internet and the Web publishing industry are relatively young, and job security with one company in the field is relatively low. Nevertheless, writers who are educated, keep up with technology, and continue to learn should not have problems finding employment.

FOR MORE INFORMATION

For ethics news and information on awards and internships, contact
Society of Professional Journalists
Eugene S. Pulliam National Journalism Center
3909 North Meridian Street
Indianapolis, IN 46208
Tel: 317-927-8000
Email: questions@spj.org
http://www.spj.org

For additional information regarding online writing and journalism, check out the following websites:
Online News Association
PO Box 30702
Bethesda, MD 20824

Tel: 617-698-5252
http://www.onlinenewsassociation.org

Visit the following website for comprehensive information on journalism careers, summer programs, and college journalism programs:
High School Journalism
http://www.highschooljournalism.org

Online Producers

QUICK FACTS

School Subjects
Art
Computer Science
English

Personal Skills
Helping/teaching
Leadership/management

Work Environment
Primarily indoors
Primarily one location

Minimum Education Level
Bachelor's degree

Salary Range
$26,490 to $44,620 to
$82,070

Certification or Licensing
None available

Outlook
Faster than the average

DOT
131

GOE
01.03.01

NOC
5123

O*NET-SOC
27-3022.00

OVERVIEW

Online producers are responsible for organizing and presenting information that is available on websites. They edit and/or write news stories, arrange the text, and any accompanying photos for online publication. They sometimes work with other workers to incorporate slideshows, background music, or audio interviews to better complement a story. While many online producers are employed in journalism, a growing number of producers find work managing corporate websites for advertising agencies, employment firms, pharmaceutical companies, nonprofits, and other organizations. Online producers are also referred to as *content producers* and *online editors*.

HISTORY

The manner in which people receive news and other information has changed with the popularity of computers and access to the Internet. People crave news—from breaking stories to real-time baseball scores—and are no longer willing to wait until the next morning's edition of their favorite newspaper to stay up to speed with the world around them. Also, portable computers and PDAs made access to the Internet possible while commuting to and from work. Web-based editions of newspapers, television stations, magazines, and radio stations have quickly found an audience. Online producers, professionals with writing and editing skills, as well as computer savvy, are needed to maintain these sites with well-written and -presented articles. Additionally, online producers are in demand in nonjournalistic settings as many businesses and other organizations seek a place on the Internet.

THE JOB

Online producers working in journalism are responsible for the daily writing/editing and presentation of information appearing on their organizations' websites. Most forms of media—newspapers, magazines, television, and radio—have a Web-based equivalent where people can access news and information on a 24-hour basis. Online producers take news articles originally published in that day's paper or broadcast and translate them into appropriate content for the organization's website. If new developments have occurred since the story was first printed, they are incorporated into the online version. Special coding is added to the article, most often HTML, which allows the text to be posted on a website. Links or related keywords are added so the article will show up in searches and archives.

The Web version of a story must be presented in a different way then it is on paper—text is often edited to be more concise and engaging to the reader. The layout of the entire article is key—if it doesn't grab the reader's attention, the story may be ignored by online readers. Online producers may choose to include features such as photos, video, animation, music, or art. Since space is not an issue on the Web, many articles run with sidebars, photos, and other features not originally included in the print or broadcast edition. Online producers often work with multimedia producers to create special content packages such as videos or an audio slide show—a series of photos presented with an audio voiceover—to further enhance a story. Other stories lend themselves to special art provided by different vendors. Online producers, working with the advertising and technical departments, decide on which pieces to purchase and use. Sports sections, for example, often use team rosters and statistics to complement special event coverage such as the Super Bowl, the World Series, or the Olympic Games.

On an average shift, online producers can expect to produce about two to four dozen stories. Many of the stories are filtered from the day's print edition, but some will be reported directly from the field, or from newswire services. Some online producers, especially at smaller companies, are responsible for producing all news stories, regardless of subject. Online producers employed at large media companies may be assigned a specific beat or area of expertise such as world news or sports. Teamwork is part of the job as well. When an important story unfolds or a special edition is being created to cover a major event—such as the death of a religious leader or a presidential election—online producers will work with other members of the editorial staff to get the news posted as quickly as possible.

Online producers also work in the corporate world at companies that range from advertising agencies to national retail chains. Producers employed in this capacity deal more with the design and maintenance of the website, or in some cases, multiple sites. An online producer working on a retail website coordinates with the company's creative merchandising team to launch a new product line or shopping portal. They monitor the site to make sure links are working properly and troubleshoot any problems. Online producers working for a school or professional organization may be responsible for setting up and moderating forums and chat rooms as well as creating online banners, online company newsletters, and posting relevant news articles regarding their employer.

REQUIREMENTS

High School
Solid computer skills will give you the edge over other candidates. Prepare yourself by enrolling in every computer class your school has to offer, from programming to website design. Familiarize yourself with different software programs such as Adobe Photoshop, DreamWeaver, or Homesite and different markup languages such as HTML. Round out your education with classes such as business, math, and English. Since many online producers have a journalism background, you'll need strong reporting, writing, and editing skills to keep up with the competition. Any classes that require written reports as regular assignments are wise choices.

Postsecondary Training
While there are many routes of study in preparation for this career, many online producers enter the field after earning a bachelor's degree in journalism. In fact, many schools now offer Web-based media classes as an elective to their traditional journalism studies. Northwestern University's Medill School of Journalism, for example, now offers a New Media concentration alongside traditional print, broadcast, and magazine journalism curricula at the undergraduate and graduate level. Besides the demands of good reporting and writing, New Media students are taught various computer languages, publishing software, and interactive tools needed to present news online, as well as how to address the challenges of instant, space unlimited publishing. Check out Medill's website

(http://www.medill.northwestern.edu/journalism/newmedia/index. html) for more information.

Other Requirements

Do you perform well under pressure? Can you quickly change gears and focus on a completely different project without complaining or losing momentum? Are you self-motivated and an independent worker, yet capable of being a team player? If you answer yes to these questions, you have some of the skills that are necessary for success in this industry.

EXPLORING

Creating your own website is an excellent way to explore this career. Not only will you gain experience in Web design, coding, and different software programs, you'll have total editorial control.

Does your school paper have a website? If not, take the initiative and build one. As online producer for this project, you can add photo slideshows of the school prom, add a team roster graphic for the winning basketball team, and spice up your site with links to school clubs and organizations.

You should also surf the Web to view existing news and corporate websites. Write down what you like and dislike about each. Are the links relevant? Is the story portrayed in a concise, yet informative manner? If given the chance, what improvements would you make?

You might also consider becoming a student member of the Online News Association, a professional organization for online journalism professionals. Besides presenting the latest industry news, the association's website offers a wealth of information on available internships, school programs, conferences, and forums. Visit http://journalist.org/about/archives/000128.php for more information regarding a membership at the student level.

STARTING OUT

A job as an assistant or associate online producer is a common starting point for this career. Many companies hiring online producers require at least three years experience in Web journalism. Internships are your best bet to gain experience and training as well as valuable industry contacts for the future.

Check with you school's career counselor for possible leads on summer internships; some publications or companies may hire high school students. Even if you spend your working day running for coffee or answering phones, at least you'll be in the company of industry professionals. Contact your local newspaper to see if any part-time employment opportunities are available during the school year or summer vacation.

Also, check with associations for job leads. The Online News Association posts job openings nationwide. Poynter Online (http://www.poynter.org/default.asp), in addition to being a great resource of industry news, offers seminars, fellowships, tip sheets, and links to employment possibilities.

ADVANCEMENT

Larger publications promote experienced online producers to senior or executive status. Those employed at regional publications could seek jobs at larger publications with broader news coverage. Online producers working in the corporate realm could advance their careers by working for larger, more diverse companies, or those with multiple websites.

EARNINGS

Although no specific salary statistics are available for online producers, earnings for these professionals are generally similar to that of traditional editors—although online editors may earn slightly more than their print counterparts. According to the U.S. Department of Labor, the median yearly income of traditional newspaper editors was $44,620 in 2004. The lowest 10 percent of all editors earned less than $26,490; the highest 10 percent earned more than $82,070. Online producers typically receive benefits such as vacation and sick days and health insurance.

WORK ENVIRONMENT

Online producers—especially those in journalism—work in hectic, fast-paced environments. Deadlines are short and may come at any time of the day or night. Online producers must be able to drop a current project, shift gears, and quickly focus on a breaking story. Most online producers have more editorial control as opposed to editors on the print side of a publication. Since much of their work is done after editorial offices have closed for the day, they often make key decisions on what stories are posted at the organization's website.

Websites operate 24-hours a day, seven days a week. News is often posted minutes after it has occurred. Work shifts are scheduled to accommodate this and may vary from week to week. Nontraditional work hours can be physically exhausting and, at times, affect an online producer's personal life.

OUTLOOK

The Web has already had a major impact on how people receive and access their news and information. And with the popularity of portable computers and cell phones, and PDAs with Internet access, the number of people turning to Web-based news and information is expected to grow. Most, if not all, forms of traditional media—newspapers, magazines, and television—have a Web-based counterpart. And with more corporate, small business, and professional organizations seeking a presence on the Web, the need for capable online producers is certain to increase.

Industry experts predict that some duties of online producers, such as story production and layout, may be eventually automated, leaving producers more time for original reporting in the field. Also, look for online producers to enjoy increasing opportunities with startup online publications that do not have ties to a print or broadcast entity.

FOR MORE INFORMATION

For information on its New Media program, contact
Medill School of Journalism
Northwestern University
845 Sheridan Road
Evanston, IL 60208-2101
Tel: 847-467-1882
Email: medill-admis@northwestern.edu
http://www.medill.northwestern.edu/journalism/newmedia/
    index.html

For information on internships, school programs, and memberships, contact
Online News Association
PO Box 30702
Bethesda, MD 20824
Tel: 617-698-5252
http://www.onlinenewsassociation.org

For information on fellowships, seminars, and employment opportunities, visit
Poynter Online
http://www.poynter.org/default.asp

─────────────── **INTERVIEW** ───────────────

Jigsha Desai is a senior online producer at the Knoxville News Sentinel *in Knoxville, Tennessee. She was kind enough to discuss her career with the editors of* Careers in Focus: Internet.

Q. What are your primary responsibilities as an online producer?

A. My primary responsibilities are:
- updating the website with newspaper content and as news breaks
- working on long-term or feature projects while performing daily duties
- performing site maintenance such as ensuring content is relevant to the day or season, links are working, images and graphics are displaying correctly
- responding to user emails and calls
- going out in the field to take photos or record video or audio for a Web feature
- scanning the Associated Press wire for pertinent news

Q. What did you study in college, and do you feel it prepared you for your career?

A. I studied journalism at Temple University in Philadelphia, Pennsylvania, and toward the end of my schooling, I took a concentration in new media.

I don't think it prepared me for my career. Most of what I know about being an online producer I learned from internships or on the job. I learned HTML when I was the online editor of my school newspaper and dabbled in Flash at a class in college. But everything about editing photos, creating a graphic, producing a package online, I learned on my internships or while on the job.

Q. How/where did you get your first job as an online producer?

A. I gradated college in May 2002 and was a Dow Jones Copy Editing Intern in Washington, D.C., for the summer. After that, I moved to Georgia where my parents were. I went to an American

Society of Newspaper Editors job fair in Nashville, Tennessee, in the early fall of 2002, where I interviewed with recruiters and editors. *The Knoxville News Sentinel* managing editor at the time took my resume, and in a week or so, I received an email from the managing editor for multimedia to come up for an interview. A week or so after the interview, I was offered the job.

Q. What are the most important personal and professional qualities for online producers?
A. Be a team player. Be a quick learner. Adapt real quickly. Have an interest in everything. Be willing to jump right in and start experimenting with your methodology and work to get good results. Be willing to ask questions and use whatever resources you have available for help. You boss won't be holding your hand, as you are likely to know more about the software and equipment being used than your boss.

Q. What are some of the pros and cons of your job?
A. Pros:
- Work in this career is always new and exciting. You're never stuck doing the same thing everyday.
- You get to work with different mediums (text, photography, audio, video, and animation).
- You're always learning.
- Since the field is so new, you have a greater chance of creating something innovative, which is always exciting.

Cons:
- You sometimes have to learn things very quickly so you can get your job done. Therefore, you only learn what you need to know at times, and not what is good to know.
- The print news side sometimes thinks you can do everything at a short time; they don't understand the way content is created on the Web.
- The changing schedule (working both nights and days) can affect your health and deprive you of sleep.
- Sometimes, you may be the most knowledgeable person in your department, even though your experience or knowledge is relatively limited.

Q. What advice would you give high school students who are interested in becoming online producers?
A. Internships are great. Build your own website. Browse news websites and see what they are doing. Take photography,

broadcast, editing, and reporting classes. Being a producer means you do all of this and more. Be engaged and excited about the world and be willing to learn quickly. And have fun. This job is a lot of fun, and you need to know that sometimes your idea won't work out. You need to know that your equipment won't always work, or your computer may crash, or deadlines may be brought forward.

Technical Support Specialists

OVERVIEW

Technical support specialists investigate and resolve problems in computer functioning. They listen to customer complaints, walk customers through possible solutions, and write technical reports based on these events. Technical support specialists have different duties depending on whom they assist and what they fix. Regardless of specialty, all technical support specialists must be very knowledgeable about the products with which they work and be able to communicate effectively with users from different technical backgrounds. They must be patient with frustrated users and be able to perform well under stress. Technical support is basically like solving mysteries, so support specialists should enjoy the challenge of problem solving and have strong analytical thinking skills. There are approximately 507,000 computer support specialists employed in the United States.

HISTORY

The first major advances in modern computer technology were made during World War II. After the war, it was thought that the enormous size of computers, which easily took up the space of entire warehouses, would limit their use to huge government projects. The 1950 census, for example, was computer-processed.

The introduction of semiconductors to computer technology made possible smaller and less expensive computers. Businesses began adapting computers to their operations as early as 1954. Within 30

QUICK FACTS

School Subjects
Computer science
English
Mathematics

Personal Skills
Helping/teaching
Technical/scientific

Work Environment
Primarily indoors
Primarily one location

Minimum Education Level
Some postsecondary training

Salary Range
$24,250 to $40,650 to
$68,720

Certification or Licensing
Recommended

Outlook
Faster than the average

DOT
033

GOE
02.06.01

NOC
6221

O*NET-SOC
15-1041.00

years, computers had revolutionized the way people work, play, and go shopping. Today, computers are everywhere, from businesses of all kinds to government agencies, charitable organizations, and private homes. Over the years, technology has continued to shrink computer size and increase speed at an unprecedented rate.

Technical support has been around since the development of the first computers for the simple reason that, like all machines, computers always experience problems at one time or another. Several market phenomena explain the increase in demand for competent technical support specialists. First of all, as more and more companies enter the computer hardware, software, and peripheral market, the intense competition to win customers has resulted in many companies offering free or reasonably priced technical support as part of the purchase package. A company uses its reputation and the availability of a technical support department to differentiate its products from those of other companies, even though the tangible products like a hard drive, for example, may actually be physically identical. Second, personal computers have entered private homes in large numbers, and the sheer quantity of users has risen so dramatically that more technical support specialists are needed to field their complaints. Third, technological advances hit the marketplace in the form of a new processor or software application so quickly that quality assurance departments cannot possibly identify all the glitches in programming beforehand. Finally, given the great variety of computer equipment and software on the market, it is often difficult for users to reach a high proficiency level with each individual program. When they experience problems, often due to their own errors, users call on technical support to help them. The goal of many computer companies is to release a product for sale that requires no technical support, so that the technical support department has nothing to do. Given the speed of development, however, this is not likely to occur anytime soon.

THE JOB

It is relatively rare today to find a business that does not rely on computers for at least something. Some use them heavily and in many areas: daily operations, such as employee time clocks; monthly projects, such as payroll and sales accounting; major reengineering of fundamental business procedures, such as form automation in government agencies, insurance companies, and banks; and issues with website performance or Internet transactions. As more companies become increasingly reliant on computers, it becomes increasingly critical that they function properly all the time. Any computer downtime can be extremely expensive, in terms of work left undone and sales not made, for example. When employees experience problems with their computer system, they call technical support for help. Technical support specialists investigate and resolve problems in computer functioning.

Technical support can generally be broken up into at least three distinct areas, although these distinctions vary greatly with the nature, size, and scope of the company. The three most prevalent areas are user support, technical support, and microcomputer support. Most technical support specialists perform some combination of the tasks explained below.

The jobs of technical support specialists vary according to whom they assist and what they fix. Some specialists help private users exclusively; others are on call to a major corporate buyer. Some work with computer hardware and software or Internet applications, while others help with printer, modem, and fax problems. *User support specialists,* also known as *help desk specialists,* work directly with users themselves, who call when they experience problems. The support specialist listens carefully to the user's explanation of the precise nature of the problem and the commands entered that seem to have caused it. Some companies have developed complex software that allows the support specialist to enter a description of the problem and wait for the computer to provide suggestions about what the user should do.

The initial goal is to isolate the source of the problem. If user error is the culprit, the technical support specialist explains procedures related to the program in question, whether it is a graphics, database, word processing, or printing program. If the problem seems to lie in the hardware or software, the specialist asks the user to enter certain commands in order to see if the computer makes the appropriate response. If it does not, the support specialist is closer to isolating the cause. The support specialist consults supervisors, programmers, and others in order to outline the cause and possible solutions.

Some technical support specialists who work for computer companies are mainly involved with solving problems whose cause has been determined to lie in the computer system's operating system, hardware, or software. They make exhaustive use of resources, such as colleagues or books, and try to solve the problem through a variety of methods, including program modifications and the replacement of certain hardware or software.

Technical support specialists employed in the information systems departments of large corporations do this kind of troubleshooting as well. They also oversee the daily operations of the various computer systems in the company. Sometimes they compare the system's work capacity to the actual daily workload in order to determine if upgrades are needed. In addition, they might help out other computer professionals in the company with modifying commercial software for their company's particular needs.

Microcomputer support specialists are responsible for preparing computers for delivery to a client, including installing the operating system and desired software. After the unit is installed at the customer's location, the support specialists might help train users on appropriate procedures and answer any questions they have. They help diagnose problems that occur, transferring major concerns to other technical support specialists.

All technical support work must be well documented. Support specialists write detailed technical reports on every problem they work on. They try to tie together different problems on the same software, so programmers can make adjustments that address all of the issues. Record keeping is crucial because designers, programmers, and engineers use technical support reports to revise current products and improve future ones. Some support specialists help write training manuals. They are often required to read trade magazines and company newsletters in order to keep up to date on their products and the field in general.

REQUIREMENTS

High School

A high school diploma is a minimum requirement for technical support specialists. Any technical courses you can take, such as computer science, schematic drawing, or electronics, can help you develop the logical and analytical thinking skills necessary to be successful in this field. Courses in math and science are also valuable for this reason. Since technical support specialists have to deal with both computer programmers on the one hand and computer users who may not know anything about computers on the other, you should take English and speech classes to improve your communications skills, both verbal and written.

Postsecondary Training

Technical support is a field as old as computer technology itself, so it might seem odd that postsecondary programs in this field are not more common or standardized. The reason behind this situation is relatively simple: formal education curricula cannot keep up with the changes, nor can they provide specific training on individual products. Some large corporations might consider educational background, both as a way to weed out applicants and to insure a certain level of proficiency. Most major computer companies, however, look for energetic individuals who demonstrate a willingness and ability to learn new things quickly and who have general computer knowledge. These employers count on training new support specialists themselves.

Individuals interested in pursuing a job in this field should first determine what area of technical support appeals to them the most and then honestly assess their level of experience and knowledge. Large corporations often prefer to hire people with an associate degree and some experience. They may also be impressed with commercial certification in a computer field, such as networking. However, if they are hiring from within the company, they will probably weigh experience more heavily than education when making a final decision.

Employed individuals looking for a career change may want to commit themselves to a program of self-study in order to be qualified for technical support positions. Many computer professionals learn a lot of what they know by playing around on computers, reading trade magazines, and talking with colleagues. Self-taught individuals should learn how to effectively demonstrate knowledge and proficiency on the job or during an interview. Besides self-training, employed individuals should investigate the tuition reimbursement programs offered by their company.

High school students with no experience should seriously consider earning an associate degree in a computer-related technology. The degree shows the prospective employer that the applicant has attained a certain level of proficiency with computers and has the intellectual ability to learn technical processes, a promising sign for success on the job.

There are many computer technology programs that lead to an associate degree. A specialization in personal computer support and administration is certainly applicable to technical support. Most computer professionals eventually need to go back to school to earn a bachelor's degree in order to keep themselves competitive in the job market and prepare themselves for promotion to other computer fields.

Certification or Licensing

Though certification is not an industry requirement, it is highly recommended. According to the Help Desk Institute, most individuals wishing to qualify to work in a support/help desk environment will need to obtain certification within a month of being on the job. A number of organizations offer several different types of certification. The Computing Technology Industry Association, for example, offers the "A+" certification for entry-level computer service technicians. Help Desk Institute has training courses and offers a number of certifications for those working in support and help desk positions. The Service and Support Professionals Association also offers certification to technical support specialists.

To become certified, you will need to pass a written test and in some cases may need a certain amount of work experience. Although going through the certification process is voluntary, becoming certified will most likely be to your advantage. It will show your commitment to the profession as well as your level of expertise. In addition, certification may qualify you for certain jobs and lead to new employment opportunities.

Other Requirements

To be a successful technical support specialist, you should be patient, enjoy challenges of problem solving, and think logically. You should work well under stress and demonstrate effective communication skills. Working in a field that changes rapidly, you should be naturally curious and enthusiastic about learning new technologies as they are developed.

EXPLORING

If you are interested in becoming a technical support specialist, you should try to organize a career day with an employed technical support specialist. Local computer repair shops that offer technical support service might be a good place to contact. Otherwise, you should contact major corporations, computer companies, and even the central office of your school system.

If you are interested in any computer field, you should start working and playing on computers as much as possible; many working computer professionals became computer hobbyists at a very young age. You can surf the Internet, read computer magazines, and join school or community computer clubs.

You might also attend a computer technology course at a local technical/vocational school. This would give you hands-on exposure to typical technical support training. In addition, if you experience problems with your own hardware or software, you should call technical support, paying close attention to how the support specialist handles the call and asking as many questions as the specialist has time to answer.

EMPLOYERS

Technical support specialists work for computer hardware and software companies, as well as in the information systems departments of large corporations and government agencies. There are approximately 507,000 technical support specialists employed in the United States.

STARTING OUT

Most technical support positions are considered entry level. They are found mainly in computer companies and large corporations. Individuals interested in obtaining a job in this field should scan the classified ads for openings in local businesses and may want to work with an employment agency for help finding out about opportunities. Since many job openings are publicized by word of mouth, it is also very important to speak with as many working computer professionals as possible. They tend to be aware of job openings before anyone else and may be able to offer a recommendation to the hiring committee.

If students of computer technology are seeking a position in technical support, they should work closely with their school's career services office. Many employers inform career services offices at nearby schools of openings before ads are run in the newspaper. In addition, career services office staffs are generally very helpful with resume and interviewing techniques.

If an employee wants to make a career change into technical support, he or she should contact the human resources department of the company or speak directly with appropriate management. In companies that are expanding their computing systems, it is often helpful for management to know that current employees would be interested in growing in a computer-related direction. They may even be willing to finance additional education.

ADVANCEMENT

Technical support specialists who demonstrate leadership skills and a strong aptitude for the work may be promoted to supervisory positions within technical support departments. Supervisors are responsible for the more complicated problems that arise, as well as for some administrative duties such as scheduling, interviewing, and job assignments.

Further promotion requires additional education. Some technical support specialists may become commercially certified in computer networking so that they can install, maintain, and repair computer networks. Others may prefer to pursue a bachelor's degree in computer science, either full time or part time. The range of careers available to college graduates varies widely. *Software engineers* analyze industrial, business, and scientific problems and develop software programs to handle them effectively. *Quality assurance engineers* design automated quality assurance tests for new software applications. *Internet quality assurance specialists* work specifically with testing and developing companies' websites. *Computer systems programmer/analysts* study the broad computing picture for a company or a group of companies in order to determine the best way to organize the computer systems.

There are limited opportunities for technical support specialists to be promoted into managerial positions. Doing so would require additional education in business but would probably also depend on the individual's advanced computer knowledge.

EARNINGS

Technical support specialist jobs are plentiful in areas where clusters of computer companies are located, such as northern California and Seattle, Washington. Median annual earnings for technical support specialists were $40,650 in 2004, according to the U.S. Department of Labor. The highest 10 percent earned more than $68,720, while the lowest 10 percent earned less than $24,250. Those who have more education, responsibility, and expertise have the potential to earn much more.

Technical support specialists earned the following mean annual salaries by industry in 2004 (according to the U.S. Department of Labor): computer and peripheral equipment manufacturing, $60,340; software publishers, $51,060; management of companies and enterprises, $46,240; computer systems design services, $45,910; colleges and universities, $39,490; and elementary and secondary schools, $38,340.

Most technical support specialists work for companies that offer a full range of benefits, including health insurance, paid vacation, and sick leave. Smaller service or start-up companies may hire support specialists on a contractual basis.

WORK ENVIRONMENT

Technical support specialists work in comfortable business environments. They generally work regular, 40-hour weeks. For certain products, however, they may be asked to work evenings or weekends or at least be on call during those times in case of emergencies. If they work for service companies, they may be required to travel to clients' sites and log overtime hours.

Technical support work can be stressful, since specialists often deal with frustrated users who may be difficult to work with. Communication problems with people who are less technically qualified may also be a source of frustration. Patience and understanding are essential for handling these problems.

Technical support specialists are expected to work quickly and efficiently and be able to perform under pressure. The ability to do this requires thorough technical expertise and keen analytical ability.

OUTLOOK

The U.S. Department of Labor predicts that the technical support specialist position will grow faster than the average for all occupations through 2012. Each time a new computer product is released on the market or another system is installed, there will be problems, whether from user error or technical difficulty. Therefore, there will always be a need for technical support specialists to solve the problems. Since technology changes so rapidly, it is very important for these professionals to keep up to date on advances. They should read trade magazines, surf the Internet, and talk with colleagues in order to know what is happening in the field. Job growth will be weaker than growth during the previous decade as many technical support jobs are being outsourced overseas.

Since some companies stop offering technical support on old products or applications after a designated time, the key is to be technically flexible. This is important for another reason as well. While the industry as a whole will require more technical support specialists in the future, it may be the case that certain computer companies go out of business. It can be a volatile industry for start-ups or young companies dedicated to the development of one product. Technical support specialists interested in working for computer companies should therefore consider living in areas in which many such companies are clustered. In this way, it will be easier to find another job if necessary.

FOR MORE INFORMATION

For information on internships, scholarships, student membership, and the student magazine Crossroads, *contact*

Association for Computing Machinery
1515 Broadway
New York, NY 10036
Tel: 800-342-6626
http://www.acm.org

For salary surveys and other information, contact
Association of Support Professionals
122 Barnard Avenue
Watertown, MA 02472-3414
Tel: 617-924-3944
http://www.asponline.com

For information on certification, contact
Computing Technology Industry Association
1815 South Meyers Road, Suite 300
Oakbrook Terrace, IL 60181-5228
Tel: 630-678-8300
http://www.comptia.org

*For more information on this organization's training courses and
certification, contact*
Help Desk Institute
102 South Tejon, Suite 1200
Colorado Springs, CO 80903
Tel: 800-248-5667
Email: support@thinkhdi.com
http://www.thinkhdi.com

*For information on careers, scholarships, student membership, and
the student newsletter* looking.forward, *contact*
IEEE Computer Society
1730 Massachusetts Avenue, NW
Washington, DC 20036-1992
Tel: 202-371-0101
http://www.computer.org

For information on certification, check out the following website:
Service and Support Professionals Association
11031 Via Frontera, Suite A
San Diego, CA 92127
Tel: 858-674-5491
Email: info@thesspa.com
http://www.thesspa.com

Webmasters

OVERVIEW

Webmasters design, implement, and maintain websites for corporations, educational institutions, not-for-profit organizations, government agencies, or other institutions. Webmasters should have working knowledge of network configurations, interface, graphic design, software development, business, writing, marketing, and project management. Because the function of a webmaster encompasses so many different responsibilities, the position is often held by a team of individuals in a large organization.

HISTORY

The Internet developed from ARPA-NET, an experimental computer network established in the 1960s by the U.S. Department of Defense. By the late 1980s, the Internet was being used by many government and educational institutions.

The World Wide Web was the brainchild of physicist Tim Berners-Lee. Although Berners-Lee formed his idea of the Web in 1989, it was another four years before the first Web browser (Mosaic) made it possible for people to navigate the Web simply. Businesses quickly realized the commercial potential of the Web and soon developed their own websites.

No one person or organization is in charge of the Internet and what's on it. However, each website needs an individual, or team of workers, to gather, organize, and maintain online data. These specialists, called webmasters, manage sites for businesses of all sizes, nonprofit organizations, schools, government agencies, and private individuals.

THE JOB

There is no definitive job description for webmasters. Many of their job responsibilities depend on the goals and needs of the particular organization for which they work. There are, however, some basic duties that are common to almost all webmasters.

Webmasters, specifically site managers, first secure space on the Web for the site they are developing. This is done by contracting with an Internet service provider. The provider serves as a sort of storage facility for the organization's online information, usually charging a set monthly fee for a specified amount of megabyte space. The webmaster may also be responsible for establishing a uniform resource locator, or URL, for the website he or she is developing. The URL serves as the site's online "address" and must be registered with InterNIC, the Web URL registration service.

The webmaster is responsible for developing the actual website for his or her organization. In some cases, this may involve actually writing the text content of the pages. More commonly, however, the webmaster is given the text to be used and is merely responsible for programming it in such a way that it can be displayed on a Web page. In larger companies webmasters specialize in content, adaptation, and presentation of data.

In order for text to be displayed on a Web page, it must be formatted using hypertext markup language (HTML). HTML is a system of coding text so that the computer that is "reading" it knows how to display it. For example, text could be coded to be a certain size or color or to be italicized or boldface. Paragraphs, line breaks, alignment, and margins are other examples of text attributes that must be coded in HTML.

Although it is less and less common, some webmasters code text manually, by actually typing the various commands into the body of the text. This method is time consuming, however, and mistakes are easily made. More often, webmasters use a software program that automatically codes text. Some word processing programs, such as WordPerfect, even offer HTML options.

Along with coding the text, the webmaster must lay out the elements of the website in such a way that it is visually pleasing, well organized, and easy to navigate. He or she may use various colors, background patterns, images, tables, or charts. These graphic elements can come from image files already on the Web, software clip art files, or images scanned into the computer with an electronic scanner. In some cases, when an organization is using the website to promote its product or service, the webmaster may work with a marketing specialist or department to develop a page.

Some websites have several directories or "layers." That is, an organization may have several Web pages, organized in a sort of "tree," with its home page connected, via hypertext links, to other pages, which may in turn be linked to other pages. The webmaster is responsible for organizing the pages in such a way that a visitor can easily browse through them and find what he or she is looking for. Such webmasters are called *programmers* and *developers;* they are also responsible for creating Web tools and special Web functionality.

For webmasters who work for organizations that have several different websites, one responsibility may be making sure that the "style" or appearance of all the pages is the same. This is often referred to as "house style." In large organizations, such as universities, where many different departments may be developing and maintaining their own pages, it is especially important that the webmaster monitor these pages to ensure consistency and conformity to the organization's requirements. In almost every case, the webmaster has the final authority for the content and appearance of his or her organization's website. He or she must carefully edit, proofread, and check the appearance of every page.

Besides designing and setting up websites, most webmasters are charged with maintaining and updating existing sites. Most sites contain information that changes regularly. Some change daily or even hourly. Depending on his or her employer and the type of website, the webmaster may spend a good deal of time updating and remodeling the page. He or she is also responsible for ensuring that the hyperlinks contained within the website lead to the sites they should. Since it is common for links to change or become obsolete, the webmaster usually performs a link check every few weeks.

Other job duties vary, depending on the employer and the position. Most webmasters are responsible for receiving and answering email messages from visitors to the organization's website. Some webmasters keep logs and create reports on when and how often their pages are visited and by whom. Depending on the company, websites count anywhere from 300 to 1.4 billion visits, or "hits," a month. Some create and maintain order forms or online "shopping carts" that allow visitors to the website to purchase products or services. Some may train other employees on how to create or update Web pages. Finally, webmasters may be responsible for developing and adhering to a budget for their departments.

Growth in Number of Websites

Date	Number of Websites
September 1993	204
August 1996	342,081
August 2000	19,823,296
August 2005	70,392,567

Source: Hobbes Internet Timeline

REQUIREMENTS

High School

High school students who are interested in becoming a webmaster should take as many computer science classes as they can. Mathematics classes are also helpful. Finally, because writing skills are important in this career, English classes are good choices.

Postsecondary Training

A number of community colleges, colleges, and universities offer classes and certificate programs for webmasters, but there is no standard educational path or requirement for becoming a webmaster. While many have bachelor's degrees in computer science, information systems, or computer programming, liberal arts degrees, such as English, are not uncommon. There are also webmasters who have degrees in engineering, mathematics, and marketing.

Certification or Licensing

There is strong debate within the industry regarding certification. Some, mostly corporate chief executive officers, favor certification. They view certification as a way to gauge an employee's skill and Web mastery expertise. Others argue, however, that it is nearly impossible to test knowledge of technology that is constantly changing and improving. Despite the split of opinion, webmaster certification programs are available at many colleges, universities, and technical schools throughout the United States. Programs vary in length, anywhere from three weeks to nine months or more. Topics covered include client/server technology, Web development, programs, and software and hardware. The International Webmasters Association and World Organization of Webmasters also offer voluntary certification programs.

Should webmasters be certified? Though it's currently not a prerequisite for employment, certification can only enhance a candidate's chance at landing a webmaster position.

What most webmasters have in common is a strong knowledge of computer technology. Most people who enter this field are already well versed in computer operating systems, programming languages, computer graphics, and Internet standards. When considering candidates for the position of webmaster, employers usually require at least two years of experience with Internet technologies. In some cases, employers require that candidates already have experience in designing and maintaining websites. It is, in fact, most common for someone to move into the position of webmaster from another computer-related job in the same organization.

Other Requirements

Webmasters should be creative. It is important for a Web page to be well designed in order to attract attention. Good writing skills and an aptitude for marketing are also excellent qualities for anyone considering a career in website design.

Although much of the webmaster's day may be spent alone, it is nonetheless important that he or she be able to communicate and work well with others. Depending on the organization for which he or she works, the Webmaster may have periodic meetings with graphic designers, marketing specialists, online producers, writers, or other professionals who have input into the website development. In many larger organizations, there is a team of webmasters rather than just one. Although each team member works alone on his or her own specific duties, the members may meet frequently to discuss and coordinate their activities.

EXPLORING

One of the easiest ways to learn about what a webmaster does is to spend time surfing the World Wide Web. By examining a variety of websites to see how they look and operate, you can begin to get a feel for what goes into a home page.

An even better way to explore this career is to design your own personal Web page. Many Internet servers offer their users the option of designing and maintaining a personal Web page for a very low fee. A personal page can contain virtually anything that you want to include, from snapshots of friends to audio files of favorite music to hypertext links to other favorite sites.

EMPLOYERS

The majority of webmasters working today are full-time employees, according to *Interactive Week*. They are employed by Web design companies, businesses, schools or universities, not-for-profit organizations, government agencies—in short, any organization that requires a presence on the World Wide Web. Webmasters may also work as freelancers or operate their own Web design businesses.

STARTING OUT

Most people become webmasters by moving into the position from another computer-related position within the same company. Since most large organizations already use computers for various functions, they may employ a person or several people to serve as computer "specialists." If these organizations decide to develop their own websites, they frequently assign the task to one of these employees who is already experienced with the computer system. Often, the person who ultimately becomes an organization's webmaster at first just takes on the job in addition to his or her other, already established duties.

Another way that individuals find jobs in this field is through online postings of job openings. Many companies post webmaster position openings online because the candidates they hope to attract are very likely to use the Internet for a job search. Therefore, the prospective webmaster should use the World Wide Web to check job-related newsgroups. He or she might also use a Web search engine to locate openings.

ADVANCEMENT

Experienced webmasters employed by a large organization may be able to advance to the position of *online producer*. These workers supervise a team of webmasters and are responsible for every aspect of a company's presence on the Web. Others might advance by starting their own business, designing websites on a contract basis for several clients rather than working exclusively for one organization.

Opportunities for webmasters of the future are endless due to the continuing development of online technology. As understanding and use of the World Wide Web increase, there may be new or expanded job duties in the future for individuals with expertise in this field.

EARNINGS

According to Salary.com, the average salary for webmasters in 2005 was $63,738. Salaries ranged from $53,588 to $76,668. However, many webmasters move into the position from another position within their company or have taken on the task in addition to other duties. These employees are often paid approximately the same salary they were already making.

According to the National Association of Colleges and Employers, the starting salary for graduates with a bachelor's degree in computer science was $47,109 in 2003; in computer programming, $45,346; and in information sciences and systems, $38,282.

Depending on the organization for which they work, webmasters may receive a benefits package in addition to salary. A typical benefits package would include paid vacations and holidays, medical insurance, and perhaps a pension plan.

WORK ENVIRONMENT

Although much of the webmaster's day may be spent alone, it is nonetheless important that he or she be able to communicate and work well with others. Depending on the organization for which he or she works, the webmaster may have periodic meetings with graphic designers, marketing specialists, online producers, writers, or other professionals who have input into website development. In many larger organizations, there is a team of webmasters rather than just one. Although each team member works alone on his or her own specific duties, the members may meet frequently to discuss and coordinate their activities.

Because technology changes so rapidly, this job is constantly evolving. Webmasters must spend time reading and learning about new developments in online communication. They may be continually working with new computer software or hardware. Their actual job responsibilities may even change, as the capabilities of both the organization and the World Wide Web itself expand. It is important that these employees be flexible and willing to learn and grow with the technology that drives their work.

Because they don't deal with the general public, most webmasters are allowed to wear fairly casual attire and to work in a relaxed atmosphere. In most cases, the job calls for standard working hours, although there may be times when overtime is required.

OUTLOOK

According to the U.S. Department of Labor, the field of computer and data processing services is projected to be among the fastest growing industries for the next decade. As a result, the employment rate of webmasters and other computer specialists is expected to grow much faster than the average rate for all occupations through 2012. As more and more businesses, not-for-profit organizations, educational institutions, and government agencies choose to "go online," the total number of websites will grow, as will the need for experts to design them. Companies are starting to view websites not as temporary experiments, but rather as important and necessary business and marketing tools.

One thing to keep in mind, however, is that when technology advances extremely rapidly, it tends to make old methods of doing things obsolete. If current trends continue, the responsibilities of the webmaster will be carried out by a group or department instead of a single employee, in order to keep up with the demands of the position. It is possible that in the next few years, changes in technology will make the websites we are now familiar with a thing of the past. Another possibility is that, like desktop publishing, user-friendly software programs will make website design so easy and efficient that it no longer requires an "expert" to do it well. Webmasters who are concerned with job security should be willing to continue learning and using the very latest developments in technology, so that they are prepared to move into the future of online communication, whatever it may be.

FOR MORE INFORMATION

For information on training and certification programs, contact the following organizations:

International Webmasters Association
119 East Union Street, Suite F
Pasadena, CA 91103
Tel: 626-449-3709
http://www.iwanet.org

World Organization of Webmasters
9580 Oak Avenue Parkway, Suite 7-177
Folsom, CA 95630
Tel: 916-989-2933
Email: info@joinwow.org
http://www.joinwow.org

Index

Entries and page numbers in **bold** indicate major treatment of a topic.

information on 51
job, described 45–47
outlook 51
overview 45
postsecondary training 48
requirements 47–49
starting out 50
work environment 51
Disney 12
DVDs 9

E

EBONE 2
e-commerce. *See* entrepreneurs,
  Internet; Internet transaction specialists; store managers, Internet
editors, online 152
  See also online producers
Electronic Arts 7, 8, 12
electronic funds transfer (EFT) 138–
  139, 142, 145
engineers, audio 9
engineers, Internet security. *See* security
  specialists, Internet
engineers, quality assurance 172
engineers, software 172
Entertainment Software Association
  15
Entertainment Technology Center
  (ETC) 10–11
entrepreneurs, Internet 128–136
  advancement 134
  earnings 134–135
  employers 134
  exploring 133
  high school requirements 131–132
  history 128–129
  information on 136
  job, described 129–131
  outlook 135–136
  overview 128
  postsecondary training 132
  requirements 131–133
  starting out 134
  work environment 135
Erspamer, Maria 147, 148, 152
executive vice presidents 97–98
e-zines 146, 147

F

firewall 118

G

Gama Network 14
Gamasutra.com 14
Game Developer 12, 14
Game Developers Conference 13, 14
Game Jobs 12
Garriott, Richard 7
Getting Your First Five Clients (Bates)
  76
graduate assistants 29

H

hackers 117, 121, 122, 142
Harvard University 27
Help Desk Institute 65, 169, 170
help desk managers. *See* help desk representatives
help desk representatives 60–70
  advancement 68
  earnings 68–69
  employers 67
  exploring 66–67
  high school requirements 63–64
  history 60–61
  information on 70
  job, described 61–63
  outlook 69–70
  overview 60
  postsecondary training 64
  requirements 63–66
  starting out 67–68
  work environment 69
help desk specialists 167
HR Certification Institute 48
HTML (hypertext markup language)
  176
Huffington, Arianna 149
Hughes, Bill 46, 47, 49, 50, 51

I

ICANN (Internet Corporation of
  Assigned Names and Numbers) 2–3
information brokers 71–79
  advancement 76–77
  earnings 77
  employers 75–76
  exploring 75
  history 71
  information on 78–79
  job, described 72–74
  outlook 78